IN AND OUT OF COURT

BY

STUART DUNCAN

The reminiscences of a retired solicitor and employment judge

TABLE OF CONTENTS

PREFACE

The essential facts described in this book are true, but some of the details may, where I have been relying on my own memory, be incorrectly recalled.

I have been able to refer to a diary that I kept of my business trip around South America and I have been able to read my own judgments, copies of which I made at the time. Also where judgments have been reported I have been able to read those reports. Apart from these exceptions though I have been totally reliant on memory.

Throughout this work I have constantly kept in mind my continuing duty of confidentiality to each of my clients which has caused me to omit a number of recollections which might have been of interest to the reader. Where a case has been reported in the law reports or elsewhere or where no issue of confidentiality has arisen I have generally, but not always, used the client's real name. Otherwise I have invented a new name to identify the client.

Generally I have written about cases or incidents where something unusual or humorous occurred, but I have also written about those cases which contained some interesting legal point and I have also written about legal practices and procedures. This work is written primarily for the non-lawyer and I have therefore tried to explain legal points, practices and procedures in non-legal language. I hope that I have succeeded and I trust that any lawyers who read this book will be patient and put up with explanations they do not need.

This work contains information, such as extracts from my own judgments, licensed under government licence version 2.0 and I am grateful for the right to be able to quote therefrom.

In preparing a paperback version of my kindle book I have made a number of small alterations. The size is different as is the pagination.

CHAPTER ONE

Early Days

It is about 9 a.m. on Wednesday 16 November 1960 and I am standing outside Great Marlborough Street magistrates court in central London waiting for my client to arrive. I am 24 years old and, after what seemed like a never ending series of exams, I had qualified as a solicitor on 1 November 1960. This is my first case appearing for a client in open court (as distinct that is to appearing before a judge in chambers). Indeed it is the very first day on which I am entitled to do so as my practising certificate, which is an essential requirement, was issued this very day.

John Nilsson, the partner in the London law firm whose assistant I was, had rung me at home the night before and told me that I was to represent a young man who had stolen a number of books from Foyles, the well-known booksellers in Charing Cross Road. John told me that the young man (let us call him Mr Browning), having left university the previous year, was working as a teacher, but was now by no means sure that he had joined the right profession. I was also told that Mr Browning was pleading guilty to shoplifting and that a former cabinet minister, who was a family friend, was going to speak as to his good character. My task was to try and persuade the magistrates to give Mr Browning the most lenient punishment possible. Being inexperienced I had prepared a draft speech the night before based on what few facts I then knew. I had decided that the speech required two key phrases and I ended up with "an impulse of the moment" and "the year of indecision."

After a short wait Mr Browning arrives. I introduce myself and ask Mr Browning my first question: "Exactly how many books did you take?" Mr Browning's reply takes me completely by surprise. "37 altogether" he says "but some of them were not actual books but rather just sheets of music."

This qualification explained how Mr Browning could get all "the books" into one large carrier bag which I later discovered was what the prosecution were alleging. Mr Browning then tells me that he did not really enjoy teaching, that he was depressed by the situation that he had found himself in and that he took the books and sheets of music randomly. Whilst waiting for the court session to start I find a quiet corner and cross out large sections of my prepared speech. "Impulse of the moment" has to go! The former cabinet minister then arrives and, after greeting him, we all go into the court.

Mr Browning's case comes on after the court had dealt with another case. I call my character witness who says that Mr Browning is a young man with high morals and that the theft is wholly out of character. I then address the bench of three magistrates. I explain that Mr Browning had become unhappy about his choice of profession and that this had made him somewhat depressed. I say that Mr Browning felt that nobody really understood his despair and that the act of taking the books and sheets of music was in effect to draw attention to his plight. I point out that any punishment that the magistrates might impose on Mr Browning could not compare with the shame that he had already brought on himself and his family. The magistrates then withdraw to consider what sentence to impose. On their return the chairman tells me that, having taken into account all the circumstances, the bench are prepared to take pity on Mr Browning and that they will give him an absolute discharge (the closest one can get to an acquittal and the best possible result). I have always since suspected that the magistrates guessed that it was my first case and were actually taking pity on me! Needless to say Mr Browning was very pleased with the result and I do hope that he later found a job that better suited his disposition.

My father was a farmer but from an early age I knew that I would not be following in his footsteps. Apart from anything else I have never liked getting up very early in the morning and, after the initial excitement of driving a tractor had worn off, I found jobs such as harrowing an eight acre field rather boring and somewhat lonely. And as for milking cows the correct technique completely eluded me. It was not I decided the life for me.

When I was about 15 I heard a programme on the radio about psychology and finding it fascinating I went to my local library and took out a couple of books that had "psychology" in the title. I read these with great interest and a week or two later I returned to the library for more books I then read throughout my teens and twenties a large number of books about psychology, a subject which has continued to enthral me ever since. Indeed at one stage I seriously thought about becoming a psychiatrist, but I changed my mind when I realised that I would have to qualify as a doctor of medicine first. A tendency to feel faint at the sight of blood would I felt be likely to be a serious disadvantage during my studies.

The nearest I ever got to practising psychiatry was working in a mental hospital in Surrey during a university vacation. However the work I did had little glamour about it - I washed up dishes. The kitchen washing up staff consisted of three Irish ladies, confusingly each called Bridget, me and an elderly male patient who rather alarmingly had a habit of thrusting carving knives that he had just washed at the nearest wall where he told me that he believed evil spirits resided. One occasion during a break I started chatting with a hospital porter. The porter happened to ask me what my ambitions were and I told him that I was reading law at university and that I hoped to qualify as a barrister or solicitor. In return I asked the porter what his ambitions were and he said "I wish to qualify as a doctor." I thought this was commendable and told him so. At which the porter gave me a somewhat crooked smile and said "But I'll have to get out of here first!"

Although I did not after all follow a medical career, I believe that my, albeit limited, knowledge of psychology has been of great assistance in my chosen career.

When I was about 16 my father, whose advice I rarely followed, suggested that I should consider becoming a lawyer. I believe that at the time my father had just paid his solicitor a rather large bill and that he therefore considered that being a lawyer was a job with some degree of financial security. In those days I was an idealist and, in thinking of becoming an advocate which was my intention, I saw myself as a knight in shining armour riding to the rescue of a damsel in distress. Capital punishment was still then the mandatory sentence for murder so the stakes could on occasion not be any higher. I had always enjoyed solving puzzles such as crosswords, number puzzles, jigsaws etc.which I thought might indicate the sort of talent that could be applied to legal problems as well. Overall the suggestion appealed to me. For once in my life therefore I did take my father's advice and I decided to try and get a university place in due course, read law and then qualify as a barrister.

Having achieved sufficient grades at the A level exams, I applied to three universities for a place which was the practice at the time. My first choice was King's College in London and I was very relieved when they were the first to respond and positively so. In October 1954 I went to stay with my uncle and aunt at their house in the Marylebone area of London and thus began my university life. I revelled in my new found freedom, but fortunately not to the prejudice of my studies. Looking back I realise that I must have developed some cultivated friends at college because it was at this stage of my life that I formed an interest in opera, ballet and the theatre. I spent many days queuing for theatre tickets whilst being entertained by buskers. A lot of theatres in those days used to provide small folding seats set out in neat rows on the pavements for those queuing which did though make it less tiring.

The first opera I saw, sitting in "the gods" at Covent Garden, was Verdi's "La Traviata." It was on this occasion sung in English rather than Italian. At one point the butler came on stage with a silver tray in his hand. "I have a letter for you" he sang in a deep voice. "You have a letter for me" was the soprano's high pitched reply. This was too much for me and I regret to say that I laughed out loud. I was quite properly told to hush by other more discerning members of the audience and I sat there with a somewhat red face. Who would have thought that I would then go on to become an opera buff.

To my surprise I also found ballet very entertaining and stimulating. I was lucky in that my first visit to the ballet was again at Covent Garden and that the ballet was "Swan Lake." I recall now how enchanted I was by the whole experience. After the performance I returned to my hostel in Camberwell and, after leaving my bus and seeing that the street I was in was empty, I decided to perform an entrechat (jumping in the air and crossing ones legs back and forth). I accordingly leapt in the air and crossed my legs once which caused them to lock and me to crash to the ground. As I ruefully pulled myself to my feet a policeman who appeared from nowhere said "And what do you think you are doing sonny?" "I was just trying to do an entrechat" I truthfully said. What he made of this I do not know but he simply walked away shaking his head from side to side. I was clearly not in the same league as Nijinsky whose entrechat involved six crossing of his legs – amazing!

Going to the theatre was also a regular activity during my college years. My friends and I went to musicals, dramas and in particular revues such as the very popular French revue "La Plume de ma Tante", "At the Drop of a Hat" with Flanders and Swann (Have some Madeira M'dear) and "Share my

9

Lettuce" in which we came across Kenneth Williams before he became famous - he was absolutely hilarious.

Another interest that I developed at university was listening to and more particularly dancing to traditional jazz. This was the time of Humphrey Lyttelton and Chris Barber. The college itself had an excellent jazz band and I was a regular on Thursdays when I jived with a girl who was in the English department at King's. This young lady had the most amazing ability to spin once or twice at a gentle push from me. We became, I believe, fairly good and I enjoyed jiving immensely - I also found that it was a marvellous way of forgetting whatever worries one had as it required absolute concentration.

I, by way of contrast to jazz, for a while "studied" comparative religion. One of my old school friends who happened to be reading law at University College was interested in different forms of religion and he got in touch with me and persuaded me to join him and another friend to attend various types of religious service. I remember going to a Jewish service, a Catholic service and a Quakers' meeting, but the one I particularly recall was a Spiritualist service where a lady went into a trance and started passing messages to members of the congregation from their dead relatives and friends. I was sitting quietly when the lady pointed a finger at me and in a deep voice said "I have a message for you from your Uncle Bob who has recently passed over." I was just about to inform her that I did not have an Uncle Bob when the lady sitting in front of me, who had bent down to pick up her prayer book, straightened up and said "Yes, yes I have an Uncle Bob what did he say?" The answer was I recall something fairly commonplace, but it seemed to impress the lady nevertheless. This service took place in a converted office building in Holborn which I assumed that I would never have reason to visit again. Imagine my surprise therefore when at the end of my first year I found that my college had hired the same room for those such as me who were sitting part one of the Bachelor of Laws exam. Fortunately I did reasonably well in the exam despite not receiving any help from the other side.

I was always short of money whilst at college so that in the summer vacations I usually did some paid work. My first summer vacation was memorable because I got a job in Filey, Yorkshire working at Butlin's holiday camp. Sadly I was not a redcoat - indeed I wore a thin blue jacket with pyjama style trousers. My job title was dining hall porter and my role was with the other porters to assist the waitresses (40 each sitting if I recall correctly) in the enormous dining rooms. On my way up to Filey by train I read Aldous Huxley's "Brave New World" (a story about the world population that is totally controlled from birth to grave). I did not know it but this was an ideal introduction to life at Butlin's. As I approached the camp which was surrounded by high fences I heard the tannoy system announce that the Camp Controller (I am using capitals to emphasise the importance of the post) had a message for the campers. I was back in my book with a character called the "resident world controller of western Europe" and somewhat apprehensive about what was to come next, but as far as I can remember it was something of very little significance.

The job of dining hall porter was in fact very hard work with long hours, but overall it was also great fun. Most evenings I went dancing and with all the exercise I lost so much weight that when I returned home my mother said that she thought I had been to Butlin's not Belsen! One of the porter's jobs was to pull in from the kitchen a large rectangular metal container on wheels which could hold over 100 meals. We were all briefed that, although it was very difficult to start the Jackson (as it was called), we must not keep on pulling as once started it would run quite easily. The reason for this is that the previous year someone had pulled very hard to start the Jackson moving and then kept on pulling. The porter then realised that he could not stop the Jackson and he had to dive out of the way as the runaway monster crashed through an enormous plate glass window into the garden outside the dining hall. This never happened during my time, but I recall a case of a misbehaving Jackson. A porter who was leaving had a riotous party the night before his departure. The following day he was badly hung over. With eyes half shut the porter pulled the Jackson into the dining hall and plugged it in to one of the electric points. This was standard practice for hot meals, but unfortunately the porter hadn't noticed that salad was being served. The guests were not impressed with lettuce that looked like brown wrapping paper. Interestingly the waitresses worked so fast that they did not notice anything wrong until they got complaints.

I was again reminded of "Brave New World" when on my first Sunday the evening meal was interrupted by a message over the tannoy. "This is the Camp Controller" the voice said in sonorous tones. "Last night three young men were caught misbehaving in chalet line B. They are no longer with us. This is a warning to those who can't behave themselves properly." This chilling message could have come straight from Aldous Huxley's book. It did however lose some of its punch when it was repeated word for word every other Sunday for my 10 weeks stay.

In my second year at university I decided that when hopefully I had obtained my degree I would try and go on to qualify as a solicitor rather than as a barrister as I had originally intended. The main reason for this change of plan was that at that time it was very difficult to earn a living wage as a recently qualified barrister unless one had connections, which I did not. Accordingly going to the bar meant relying

12

on my father to finance me for a period of two or three years - or possibly even more - which neither of us wanted.

After getting an upper second degree, I started looking for articles (the then training system for solicitors). I particularly recall going for an interview to a firm called Scadding & Bodkin (yes that really was their name). My recollection is that their offices lived up to their Dickensian name. I believe that it was Mr Bodkin himself who interviewed me. Mr Bodkin asked me various questions about my background and my reasons for wanting to be a solicitor and then he said that he would take me on, but that we had better discuss money. "I think £500 would be about right" he said. This in those days was a substantial sum of money (over £10,000 in today's currency). And regrettably it was for me to pay the £500 to him so that I could work hard for the best part of three years whilst in theory I would receive training which was so valuable that it would exceed the value of my work by £500. I politely declined this generous offer. How things have changed since then.

I went for about half a dozen further interviews until I came to a firm called Godfrey Davis & Foster. This firm had offices in New Square which was just to the east of Lincoln's Inn Fields and conveniently just behind The Law Courts in London. I liked the partner who interviewed me, liked the location of the offices and liked the offer (financially the best I got). I was told that the firm would take me on and that, although I would receive no pay for six months, my position would then be reviewed and, if I was worthy, I would receive a weekly salary. I gratefully accepted this offer and I started working as an articled clerk on or about 1 October 1957. As I had no income of my own my father gave me an allowance of £2 per week which he thought would be sufficient for my needs. It was, but only just. I recall that I kept in a small red cash book a list of my expenditure each week to make sure that I didn't overspend. I also recall that if I took a girlfriend to the theatre and she had a gin and tonic in the interval I had no date the following week.

In the late fifties articled clerks did just about everything in a law office. Serving the tea or coffee, tidying up rooms, moving furniture or whatever. I can recall photocopying documents using, if I remember correctly, three liquids and then attaching the wet prints to a sort of washing line with clothes pegs. I never complained though because Godfrey Davis, the partner I was articled to, once told me that when he was articled he had to sweep the chimneys. Nevertheless the firm treated me very well indeed and I was given a great amount of responsibility and got really good experience. I regularly sat in on interviews with clients and as I became more experienced I regularly saw clients on my own. When I qualified I therefore had a degree of confidence that in other circumstances I would not have had.

If you were a law graduate articles of clerkship lasted three years during which you had to pass an accounts exam (usually after taking a correspondence course) and then near the end was the solicitors' final exam. This final exam covered a very wide range of legal subjects and required full time attendance for some five months at a college of law and then about a month away from the office to prepare for and sit the exam.

During my articles I lived at home which was a farm in Surrey. To get to London I had to walk over a mile, catch a bus which took about half an hour to get to East Croydon station and then board a train to Charing Cross station from where I walked or if it was raining took the tube. A quicker, albeit less conventional way, was to hitch-hike the first part of the journey. If I stood outside the farm, although I was on a country lane, I was also on a commuter route to London. I wore the traditional black suit, had a rolled up umbrella, and carried a black brief case. I suspect that the commuters stopped, as they often did, out of surprise and curiosity. All sorts of interesting people gave me a ride and I had some fascinating conversations with a variety of commuters including managing directors of large companies, bankers and occasionally lawyers. One lawyer who stopped for me (I was going to write "picked me up", but realised that the reader with knowledge of subsequent events might misunderstand) was Jeremy Thorpe. He was a television personality, a barrister and he later became leader of the Liberal Party. Many years later Jeremy Thorpe was indicted for conspiracy to murder his male lover in a famous case at the end of which he was acquitted. I however recall him as a friendly man with whom I had an interesting conversation about the techniques of advocacy.

I also recall a man who gave me a lift asking me what I was doing out in the country dressed as I was and I told him that I had recently qualified as a solicitor and that I was going for a job interview. The driver then started to criticise the legal profession generally and in particular for overcharging on conveyancing (land sales, purchases etc.). I defended my new profession stoutly. When we got to East Croydon the driver asked me if I would like him to take me into central London. I readily agreed and the attacks on the profession continued. However when the driver pulled in to Lincoln's Inn Fields I became suspicious. "Is this o.k. for you" he said "and by the way would you like to come to my firm for a more formal interview?" I realised, as I had suspected for a short time, that the driver was also a solicitor and that he had been interviewing me without my knowledge. I must have done all right though as he would not otherwise have offered me the possibility of a job. The interview that I actually attended that day was with a partner in the firm that I did in fact join. Consequently I never took up the car driver's offer. I wonder though now how different my life would have been if I had started my professional life in Lincoln's Inn Fields rather than in the nearby Clements Inn.

My father, who disliked bureaucracy, often had scrapes with the law and I recall whilst I was in articles that he was prosecuted for allowing some cows to stray on to the highway at Caterham in Surrey. I gave my father some advice and he represented himself in (I believe) Croydon magistrates court. A police officer, whom I suspect had been brought up in a town, gave evidence of seeing some 12 cows wandering down the road. My father then started to cross examine him. His first question was "Please define for me what a cow is?" The police officer was flummoxed and, after thinking for a while, said "It is a large animal with four legs and a tail that provides milk." My father then said "Would you instead accept that it is a bovine animal that has had a calf." The officer, seeing a way out of his dilemma, readily agreed. "Then I put it to you" said my father "that what you actually saw were bullocks, not cows at all." This was in fact the case and the officer had to agree. As the summons referred to "cows" my father was able to persuade the magistrates that the summons should be dismissed. You may think this anecdote is "a load of bullocks", but I assure you that it happened just as I have described.

Most of my time during articles was spent in the office (where I had a great view of the gardens in New Square - particularly beautiful in the spring when the tulips were out) or in the Royal Courts of Justice. Years later, after the firm had left its offices in New Square, I returned to the same building for a conference with a barrister and found to my nostalgic delight that his room was the same room I had occupied when I had started out on my career

Early on in my articles I do though recall a day out, accompanying one of the partners on a farm valuation. What I

- or indeed he - was doing there I do not now recall. In any event the landowner and the valuer paid me little attention which, in view of my status and lack of contribution, was fair enough. After valuing items around the farmhouse it was necessary for the valuer to visit the far stretches of the farm. It was decided that this would be done by having a tractor pull a trailer in which the landowner, the valuer and my firm's partner would sit. There was however a problem in that all the farm workers were busy in the fields. "Ah" the partner said "but my articled clerk can drive a tractor." Suddenly I was treated with new respect. It was a lovely day and as I drove along I for once thoroughly enjoyed a farming activity that I had turned my back on. Unfortunately I started day dreaming and temporarily forgot that I had a trailer behind. I took a corner too sharply and heard an anguished cry from behind. I turned around and was aghast to see that the trailer had tilted and the three men were pitched sideways, the somewhat elderly and distinguished valuer having his legs stuck up in the air. I was promptly removed from tractor driving duties and my new found respect just as promptly melted away. Indeed I was regarded with some suspicion for the rest of the day. Later my firm's partner instead of being angry with me said that he was quietly quite amused by the whole thing which was something of a relief to me.

As already mentioned my firm gave me a lot of responsibility as I grew more experienced, but nevertheless Godfrey Davis considered that I was not really senior enough to assist a barrister who was briefed to appear on a court martial to be heard in Germany. I was sorry to be overlooked because it was a very interesting case. The client, a soldier, was accused of murder and when he was in custody he had drawn a series of cartoons showing him committing the murder, sitting in his cell, being sentenced to death in court and then being hanged. Unfortunately for him our client's perception of his own future was dead right.

After six months Godfrey Davis called me in to his office and told me that the firm were happy with my progress and that I would thereafter be paid £2 per week. I was very pleased with this news, particularly as I was the only one of my year at university that I knew of who was getting any salary at all. I was however less pleased when my father cancelled my allowance. In fact I was now worse off as I had to pay national insurance contributions out of my salary.

Sometime later Godfrey Davis told me that they were very short staffed at their Mitcham office and he asked me to help out on a long term basis. I was not initially happy at this as I wanted London experience. However with reluctance I agreed. One positive aspect though was that my journey time was much reduced as Mitcham is not far from Croydon. On my first day at the new offices I remember Brian Baldwin, the partner in charge, taking me into a large room and saying "This is your office"; he then showed me a large pair of filing cabinets and said "Your files are in here" and finally he introduced me to a young lady and said "And this is your secretary." I was taken aback to say the least. It was not in those days, as far as I knew, usual for an articled clerk to have his own office, his own files and a dedicated secretary. Brian Baldwin then went back to his own office and I hardly saw him again during the first fortnight I was there as he was so busy.

My recollections of my time in Mitcham are now a little hazy, but I do recall a client who had accidentally chopped off one of his fingers in a wire cutting machine and every time he came in he insisted on showing me the stump so that I could see how it was healing. I also recall a man who always came for appointments carrying three or four plastic bags crammed to the full. I never did find out what was in them, but it may just be that he did his week's shopping on the way.

As an articled clerk in a small office I had to cover all areas of the law. One conveyancing transaction I recall with embarrassment was the purchase of a house for an important client. The day of completion was set and my job was to travel in to central London with a bankers draft and come back with the deeds. It was a busy day and I had to rush to be on time for my appointment. I arrived at the offices where completion was to take place and I met two solicitors who looked very experienced. One acted for the vendor and the other for a building society. We started the completion and I checked to see that the deeds were in order. We then got to the point where I was to hand over the money. To my dismay I then realised that I had forgotten to pick up the bankers draft. I accordingly had to ring my secretary and ask her to come up to London as quickly as possible with the missing draft. The building society solicitor and I then adjourned to the waiting room to wait. It was silent. I felt I had to say something. "Do you do many completions?" I asked. "Five or six every day" he replied. Unwisely I added "Has this ever happened to you before?" "Never" was his brusque reply. I decided that silence was after all the best option and I shut up until my secretary arrived with the bankers draft and completion then took place.

Despite my earlier reservations I thoroughly enjoyed my time at Mitcham. It was a very friendly office with a good team spirit. Because Godfrey Davis was part of our firm name it was not uncommon for people to ring up and order a car, but our receptionist who had a wry sense of humour had a standard reply which was to say that we had no cars but we could send them a conveyance! I learnt a lot at the Mitcham office about practising law and I gained considerable experience in dealing with clients on my own.

After about two and a quarter years of articles I went to a college of law for intensive study and after taking my solicitors' final exam I returned to finish my articles. However I was now asked to work in the London office which had moved to Cavendish Square. I was given a real salary (I think it was £7 per week) and I did my best to earn it. When I got the exam results and I knew that I had qualified I started looking for another job. Although I was very happy with Godfrey Davis & Batt (as they were now called) I considered that if I stayed on I would always be known as the ex-articled clerk and I preferred to be known as the new solicitor.

Before being admitted as a solicitor every articled clerk has to attend an interview at the Law Society. This was to establish whether the applicant was a gentleman (or occasionally a lady) fit to join the profession. All I can now remember of this interview was that one of the panel of three, noticing that I lived on a farm, asked me whether I shot any game. I told him that I did so and he said that he hoped that I was not currently doing so as it was off season. In fact I normally only shot pigeons and hares and I usually missed, except for the last time I ever went shooting which was when I was in my mid-twenties. I only had four cartridges left and I was shortly going to sell my gun. I told my father that I would bring him back two hares and two pigeons and about an hour later I returned with no cartridges, but I did have two hares and two pigeons. My father was so surprised that he thought that I had been to the butchers in the nearby town and I am not sure that I ever convinced him otherwise. In any event I was accepted by the Law Society panel as a fit person to become a solicitor.

Godfrey Davis, who used to sit on the Law Society's panel for approval of entrants, told me that he had sat on many interviews and had only ever failed two applicants. I asked him why these two were rejected and he told me that one had kept his hands in his pockets throughout the entire interview and appeared disinterested in the whole process and the other when asked why he wanted to be a solicitor said that he had heard that there were "good pickings." I think I would have failed those applicants as well.

I attended lots of interviews for the position of a solicitor in a litigation department (litigation is broadly the area of a solicitors' practice that is concerned with disputes which may or may not go to court or arbitration). I did not consider any other department of law as I enjoyed the buzz of the courts, despite the fact that I could only appear as an advocate in the magistrates courts and in the county courts (in the more senior courts, unless the hearing is in chambers, a barrister has to be instructed). Eventually I accepted an offer from a firm called Henry Pumfrey & Son which practised in Clements Inn, a lane along the side of The Royal Courts of Justice and not far from where I had started my legal career. The firm also had offices at Orpington in Kent. Once again I liked the partner who interviewed me (one Gordon Brown – this was before another Gordon Brown became famous so he never got teased). I also liked the location. Gordon Brown did though ask me an odd question during my interview. "Have you seen any clients?" he asked. "I am sorry but I do not know what you mean" I responded. It then became clear that Gordon Brown was asking me if I had seen any clients on my own. As this had in fact been the case throughout most of my articles I was able to assure him on this point.

My starting salary as an assistant solicitor was £600 per year. After the low income I had received over the last six years I felt I was now a wealthy man.

I worked for John Nilsson, whom I mentioned at the start of my reminiscences, and with a clerk called Adrian Wood we represented the litigation department of the London office. John was a very astute lawyer and taught me a lot. Adrian was streetwise and something of a character. I can recall one occasion when Adrian was going to a special dinner. It was very late in the day and he was changing into evening dress. When Adrian was fully attired he went to the door to find that somebody had locked the office up and he could not get out. We were, if I remember correctly, four or more storeys up. Nevertheless Adrian decided that if he got out of the window he could walk along a small ledge to another room where hopefully both window and door would be open. Smartly dressed Adrian inched along the ledge. It so happened that Raymond Pumfrey, the senior partner, was working late seeing a client in the adjoining room. The client who was facing the window suddenly saw Adrian, who instead of entering that room had wisely decided to move on to the next room. "Somebody just walked past outside the window in a dinner jacket" the astonished client said. "Oh, that was probably Adrian" said the senior partner and he continued with the interview as if nothing had happened.

Life as a litigation solicitor was very varied and in my case involved regularly appearing in court. I have described my first appearance in the magistrates court, but about two weeks thereafter I appeared for the first time in the county court dressed in a borrowed black gown with a wing collar and tabs. It was, I remember, Bromley county court, but I do not now recall what the case was about. I do though recollect that I had to rely on a deed conveying some land to prove my case. At the relevant point in the proceedings I produced the deed, but the judge looked at it and said "Before I can accept this deed in evidence it needs to be stamped to show that stamp duty has been paid and there is no such stamp on it." I then remembered one of my lecturers at the college of law saying that in such a situation the advocate could give an undertaking that after the case he would have the deed stamped if stamp duty was indeed required. I accordingly offered such an undertaking, but the judge said that he was not happy to proceed on that basis. So much for my lecturer's helpful tip! I told the judge that I did not think the deed needed a stamp, but I could not provide any authority for this proposition. The judge accordingly adjourned the case whilst he took another short case and he suggested that I ring the Stamp Office to check the position. I found a phone (no mobile phones then) and rang the Stamp Office which is a department of the government responsible for stamp duty. I explained the situation and the officer I spoke to confirmed that in the particular circumstances the deed was exempt from stamp duty. I then went back into court. The judge saw me and, interrupting the case that he was hearing, said "Have you something to say, Mr Duncan?" Sheepishly I explained the position to the judge and I was given the order I had sought. The lesson I learnt, or should have learnt, is to check every possibility before going into court.

Advocacy, I discovered, is a bit like an iceberg. Only about one ninth of the iceberg is above water and eight ninths are unseen. Likewise with advocacy eight hours preparation should prepare one for a one hour performance. In reality the ratio is not usually quite so dramatic, but the point remains good: preparation pays.

In the sixties if a debtor did not pay his debt the creditor could issue a judgment summons which required the debtor to attend a county court at which the creditor or his representative could question him as to his means whereafter an instalment order or some other order could be made. My first judgment summons was in a North London county court. I had prepared the questions I was to put on behalf of my client in advance. A standard question in those days was "Do you own a television?" If the answer was "Yes" there was a fair chance that the judge would be critical of somebody indulging in a luxury when they owed money. It is surely different today. I sat there with my file all ready to go and the usher called out the name of the debtor. I rose to my feet and introduced myself but nobody came forward. This I had not bargained for. I did not know what to do. I turned to my right and saw a grey haired solicitor. "What do I do" I said. "Ask for a 107" he replied. I looked up at the judge and said "Could I have a 107 please your honour." "What is that" said the judge. I quickly turned to my right again, but the grey haired solicitor had gone. I looked at the judge and had to explain that I did not actually know what a 107 was. I wished that the earth would swallow me up. "Shall I make an order that the debtor do attend on a future date" said the judge helpfully. I readily agreed. It was only when I got back to the office that I discovered that 107 was the number of the standard form requiring the debtor to attend court on a stated date This was accordingly another example of having to check every possibility in advance. Henry Cecil tells a similar story in one of his books - I believe it was "Brothers in Law". As the author sat as a Judge at Willesden county court I thought his salutary tale was based on my experience, but on checking I found that the book came out first. I suspect though that Henry Cecil was inspired by an incident involving another unfortunate advocate.

During these early years I regularly appeared in the county courts and the magistrates courts in London and the surrounding area. The London tube map was my constant guide and I often found myself in parts of London that hitherto were completely unknown to me. My most usual destination though was the Bear Garden - this was the colloquial name for a part of the Royal Courts of Justice which as I have previously mentioned was very close to my firm's offices. There was an open area with rooms leading off it where masters sat. The masters were in effect junior judges who made decisions on procedural matters for the most part, but they could give judgments where there was no defence put forward or the defence served lacked any merit. In my day these gentlemen (no ladies!) were a fierce lot and liked nothing better than to bark at some unfortunate advocate for his or her inadequate presentation. A number of the masters had some physical impediment and I was told (rightly or wrongly) that they had to give up lucrative careers at the bar because of this and thus they were doubly irritable when dealing with the somewhat mixed quality of advocacy that they encountered. The open area was in a sort of well overlooked by balconies and the waiting advocates down below were often seen and heard trading verbal blows with their opponents in loud tones. It did therefore in many respects resemble a bear garden.

In spite of the great experience I had gained during my articles I quickly realised in my first couple of years as a solicitor that there was a lot to learn and that nothing should ever be taken for granted. Certainly preparing for every possibility however unlikely it might be helped but even then there was still plenty of chances for things to go awry.

CHAPTER TWO

Articled Clerks

In or about 1962 the partners of Henry Pumfrey & Son decided to open a branch office just outside Croydon in Surrey and John Nilsson left the London office to head it up and get it going. As a consequence I was appointed head of the litigation department in London and I became a partner - a promotion that was somewhat earlier than I could have reasonably expected. Over the years I have had quite a number of fellow partners and I do not know if I was lucky or not but I got on very well with nearly all of them. I also had quite a number of assistant solicitors working under me and I believe that we always had a good working relationship as well. The articled clerks on the other hand were a varied lot and, although most of them were pleasant and hardworking, there were some who would have severely tested Job. I know this because throughout most of my career it was one of my particular responsibilities to give the articled clerks their first six months training.

So far I probably appear to the reader to be somewhat less than competent. However, when I look back on my life, it is not the straightforward cases that I remember but the ones that had an interesting legal point, went wrong in some way or other or had some humorous element. Accordingly I believe that the overall picture can become distorted by selection. Dispensing with modesty I believe that I was actually quite a good solicitor. I know from comparison with my colleagues that I was very well organised and I was also obsessively tidy. In fact I think that I was the tidiest solicitor that I ever met. The articled clerks were therefore sent to me first so that I could teach them in particular to keep their files neatly, to use their time efficiently, to be precise in their use of language and to be accurate and detailed in the notes they made of events or telephone conversations. Of course I also taught them how to relate to clients and the practices and procedures of the courts.

I believed in having office systems to make things run more smoothly and I recall two among a number that I introduced. The firm's files were usually kept in filing cabinets in the room of the solicitor or executive handling the matter. Generally speaking each file contained a separate instruction from a client. Accordingly if a client was selling his house and buying a new one the papers relating to each transaction would be in separate files. The files would show on the outside the name of the client and a short description of the transaction together with a short reference which was useful for precise identification in letters and on bills. If I remember correctly we had an all number reference system which I thought could be improved. I therefore introduced a reference system which used the first three letters of the client's name together with a number to indicate the name of the specific client, followed by another number to indicate the specific job. For example if John Adams was the firm's first client his case would be referenced under ADA.1-1. I take no credit for this system as I read of it in an article by a solicitor who was at university with me. I also - and this was my own idea - had different coloured files for different areas of litigation. Red was for divorce and family matters, blue was for breaches of contract and commercial disputes, orange was for accident claims, other acts of negligence and suchlike (called "tort" by lawyers), green was for criminal matters, grey was for claims involving a death and pink was for miscellaneous matters. This enabled files to be much more quickly identified when taking them out of filing cabinets and it also made for a more colourful working life.

Diverting for a moment this reminds me of a game a solicitor I once met had invented. The game called "Splitto" was based on the rules and procedures then applicable for obtaining a divorce. There were four pieces that were moved around a track set out on a board. The red piece was for the petitioner claiming cruelty (seeing red), the green piece was for the petitioner claiming adultery (green-eyed jealousy), the yellow piece was for the petitioner claiming desertion (turning yellow), and the white piece was for the petitioner claiming insanity (white coats worn in asylums). The idea was for each player to choose a piece and then it was a race to see who got their decree absolute first. The first square indicated that a solicitor had been instructed and then there were a combination of blank squares and squares marked with each successive stage of the process, such as the filing of the petition, applying for a hearing date and so on. The last square then indicated that a decree absolute of divorce had been obtained. Different squares on the track gave benefits or imposed burdens - it all depended on the roll of the dice. All I can now remember was a square that stated "Your solicitor reports that your case is going well" followed by "Go back three spaces." Clearly my friend was a man with a dry sense of humour.

Reverting to my theme, I taught the articled clerks various techniques to improve their efficiency. Most important of these perhaps was the diary system which was not in any way a ground breaking idea. Each articled clerk had to keep an office diary with a day to the page. Half the page was for appointments and half was a note of everything that in a perfect world should be done that day. Anything not done was then carried forward to the next day. Steps that had to be taken by a particular date were put in the diary some days in advance and on the final day marked with an asterisk. Two of my ex- articled clerks whom I dined with after I had retired told me that they had met at a conference and not having met each other before just happened to talk about their office practices. One apparently explained that everything was run from his diary in which he put in appointments and everything to be done that day and the other apparently said "You must have been trained by Stuart Duncan as well."

Another technique I taught the articled clerks was to think laterally in solving problems. For example, if one could not reach the end desired by taking appropriate legal action, I recommended that the articled clerk should consider alternatives such as advising the client to pay out money, move house, threaten what might be unwelcome publicity or wait and do nothing. Once when I was recently qualified I sent in a bill to a client and part of it read "After considering all possible alternatives advising you to do nothing." I thought then and still think now that this was the correct response to the problem, but the client did not care for my honesty and complained to the senior partner that we were charging him for doing nothing. After that experience my bills in similar circumstances were more oblique in their wording.

Another approach I taught which occasionally helped was to imagine the end of some procedure and then work backwards to see how one got there. With regard to writing letters to opponents I advised that my articled clerks should first ask themselves what was the purpose of their letter and secondly what sort of reply did they anticipate receiving - and then of course how they would respond to that reply. Like chess one has to think some moves ahead. With more complex letters I suggested that my articled clerks should first write down "the chapter headings" for each paragraph before starting dictation. This I told them would make a much better structured letter.

I insisted that my articled clerks wrote everything down that had occurred including every telephone conversation, however seemingly inconsequential. I practised what I preached and over forty years as a lawyer I wrote down virtually every business telephone conversation I had in longhand and put the note on the file. Sometimes I dictated a formal file note to my secretary, but not that often. If an articled clerk mentioned that he or she was told something on the telephone I would look at the file and, if there was no note, I would tell them that it had not happened.

Throughout my career I must have made or received, I calculate, something like 100,000 telephone calls. That I think is more than enough and now that I have retired if the phone rings I leave it to my wife to take the call - it's usually for her anyway. Some random memories of telephone calls include a call I made to a firm in the East End. The telephonist asked my name and I said it was Duncan. "I'll put you through Mr Dunkirk" she said. "No" I said "Duncan as in Macbeth." "I am sorry" she replied "We do not have much time for reading Macbeth in the East End." I think though she was making fun of me because she then introduced me as Mr Macbeth. On another occasion I rang a firm that had offices near the Law Courts. A lady with the most seductive voice answered and said "It's the Chancery Lane harem here, can I help you?" I was so surprised that I could not think of any witty, or indeed any appropriate, answer and simply said "I must have a wrong number." Once when our telephonists were busy I answered the phone and putting on my best telephone voice said "Henry Pumfrey & Son." The caller responded by saying "Damn it's the bloody answerphone." "No it isn't" I replied to his astonishment. I must have articulated especially well. I also recall going into the office one Saturday to work on a particular case and the phone rang. I think I was the only person there and I should have just left it to ring. In fact I picked it up and the caller said that he was going to come round and kill me. It clearly was not meant for me, but it's still somewhat chilling to receive a death threat

On the subject of telephone calls I once read of a very good way of ending a call when the caller won't stop talking -

which is not unknown with clients of a law firm. The trick is to interrupt what the caller is saying and then cut oneself off in the middle of a sentence. Nobody would ever believe that somebody would do such a thing. I tried it a few times and it worked very well.

An occasion when my practice of making a contemporaneous note proved invaluable was the case of a lady (let us call her Miss Johnson) who had a dispute over some accounts. I instructed a chartered accountant called Mr May, if I remember correctly, to review the accounts. Mr May did so and he made some corrections which I called "the May amendments." I sent a copy of the amended accounts to Miss Johnson and then rang her when she told me that she agreed the amendments and I could accordingly inform the other side's solicitors of this. I then rang those solicitors and told them that the May amendments were agreed. As I was speaking on the phone I wrote down a record of both conversations in longhand. A few days later we appeared before a master in chambers. The other solicitors came up to me beforehand and asked Miss Johnson to sign the amended accounts. Miss Johnson however refused, saying that she did not agree the May amendments and never had. This put me in a dilemma because I had agreed the amendments to the accounts with Miss Johnson's express approval. In view of this disagreement I told Miss Johnson that I could not act for her any further. In the circumstances the master decided to refer the case to a High Court judge.

Sometime later the case came up and I was called by the other solicitors to give evidence that the amendments to the accounts had in fact been agreed. In effect I was to give evidence against my ex-client. This is a pretty rare occurrence and I therefore researched into the law on this point. After my research I was satisfied that in the particular circumstances I could - indeed was obliged - to tell the court what had occurred. I entered the witness stand and started to tell the judge about the two telephone conversations. The judge however suddenly stopped me and turning to the barrister opposing Miss Johnson said "Is this not confidential, being a conversation between a client and her solicitor?" Unfortunately the barrister had not done his homework and there was something of a hiatus whilst law reports were called for and considered. I did not feel that I could tell the judge of the relevant case (Conlon v. Conlons Ltd which decided that where a client instructs a solicitor to communicate with the opposition then both the communication and the instructions are no longer confidential) as I was not surprisingly not very popular with my ex-client and did not want to make things worse. Eventually the barrister found the particular case and I was asked to continue. I started to read from my longhand note of my conversation with Miss Johnson, but the judge interrupted again. I should here explain that there is a rule that a written document recording an oral conversation cannot be referred to in evidence unless it is made at or shortly after the event. The judge said "Did you make this record shortly after the telephone conversation, Mr Duncan?" "No my Lord, I replied. "Well I am sorry" said the judge "but you cannot therefore refer to it." I then explained to the judge that my note was made as the conversation was actually taking place - a circumstance he had not considered - and I was allowed to proceed and Miss Johnson rightly lost her case.

The articled clerks, as I have already pointed out, were something of a mixed bunch. Some eventually went on to become partners in the firm, some moved on to other firms or had success elsewhere and some were not in my view cut out to be solicitors at all.

I remember the first articled clerk I helped to train generally but also for one particular reason. The firm were acting for a landlord who was assaulted by his tenant in the lavatory at Leicester Square underground station. The landlord to try and escape the assault locked himself in a cubicle and the tenant tried to force the door open until the lavatory attendant came to the landlord's aid. Clearly the lavatory attendant was a vital witness in subsequent legal proceedings and I therefore asked my articled clerk to fix up an interview with him and take a witness statement. The articled clerk accordingly wrote a letter to the lavatory attendant and asked him if he could meet him at his convenience. This is the only occasion that I have heard this standard expression used in such a literal way!

One of the many articled clerks I trained was of Irish descent (I mention this only because it may explain his literary aspirations). The articled clerk was charming, but totally unpredictable. One day I sent this articled clerk on an errand and he wrote up his attendance note on the train back. Mindful of my injunction that he should make a note of everything that had occurred he started his note along these lines: "I left the office on a beautiful day, took the tube to Waterloo and had a very pleasant journey to Wimbledon. The sun was hot and there were small puffy white clouds drifting across a bright blue sky." I would have accepted this surfeit of irrelevant information if the articled clerk had kept the tone of his note going when he came to the interview he had conducted with a potential witness, but sadly the mood left him and there was very little detail of what actually mattered.

I think it was the same unpredictable articled clerk who decided one day that he would provide the litigation department secretaries with coffee (not his job). The articled clerk put five cups of coffee on a tray and with some skill safely negotiated the stairs. When the articled clerk reached the room where the secretaries worked he found that their door was shut, so he put the tray on his head and opened the door. The secretaries looked up and admiring his balancing ability clapped. Up to that point all was well, but our hero then made a fatal mistake - he took a bow. The tray not surprisingly slipped out of his hands and the coffee inevitably poured down the front of his suit.

Another articled clerk one day accompanied me on a conference with a barrister. After the conference I was going directly to the opera and I asked the articled clerk to take my brief case home with him and bring it back the next day. I stressed that the action was shortly coming up for trial and that all the relevant papers were in the briefcase. Next day I decided to prepare the brief to counsel (written instructions accompanied by copies of all the relevant papers) and I asked the articled clerk for my briefcase. The articled clerk coolly answered that he had left it on the tube, but it was all right because he would buy me another. To say that I was furious would be an understatement. I realised that if the briefcase was not found I would somehow have to reconstruct the entire file (no computers then). I waited until the last possible moment when to my intense relief the briefcase was found and returned. The articled clerk then said that all was well and I need not have worried. I had to bite my tongue and clench my fists. After about five months of having my patience stretched to breaking point, the articled clerk in question told me that one of his parents was unwell and that, although he was sorry to let me down, he would have to return to his parents' home which happened to be some considerable distance from London. He said that he would have to give up his articles. I told him that I was sorry about his bad news, but I must admit that I was in fact somewhat relieved.

Two incidents I remember involved articled clerks and photographs. I was acting in a custody case, if I recall correctly, and I believed that the wife of my client was about to leave the country with her lover. It was important to serve a court order on her and I instructed one of my articled clerks to do this. We believed that the lady was staying in a London hotel and the articled clerk went there one dark evening carrying a very large wedding photograph which was all I had by way of identification. As the articled clerk arrived a car started to pull away from the front of the hotel. My articled clerk saw a blonde lady in the front passenger seat and believing it was his quarry threw himself in front of the car. The driver slammed on the brakes narrowly avoiding the abrupt termination of my colleague's articles. "You damned idiot" he shouted in an American accent to which the lady added in a like accent "Are you mad?" My client's wife was not American and my articled clerk realised his mistake; he felt that he had to say something and in a faltering voice said "Do you know where Great Portland street is?" The two Americans were no doubt by now confirmed in their belief that my articled clerk was indeed crazy.

The other incident involving photographs concerned a client who had not paid her bill. I asked an articled clerk to serve a writ on her. "How will I recognize her?" he said. I told him that there was a sheet in the file with various photographs of the client from which he could identify her. Off the articled clerk went to some other part of London and on his return I asked him how he had got on. He said "You did not tell me she was a nude model - I barely recognised her with her clothes on." In any event the articled clerk had managed to serve the writ on the lady that he had met and fortunately she was indeed the non-playing client.

Articles of clerkship have now been replaced by training contracts and because the trainees get fairly well paid there is no longer such scope for sending them on the type of missions that I have described. I personally believe that something has been lost in the process. Encouraging the young to use their initiative and letting them see the consequences of their actions is also important. Being a solicitor in my view, as well as being a serious job, should also be an adventure, laced with drama and humour. I wonder how true that is of the modern solicitor's life.

In or about 1967 my firm merged with Stoneham & Sons who had their practice in Cannon Street in the City. Stoneham & Sons, although not a large firm, had a significant international practice. The firm had opened a branch office in Portugal and had contacts in law firms worldwide. The head of the Lisbon office was an English barrister and when The Law Society found this out they insisted on severance (it was not permitted for solicitors and barristers to be partners). This took place before the merger, but nevertheless a strong bond remained between London and Lisbon.

As is not unusual in merger negotiations one of the knotty issues was the name of the new firm. Both senior partners wanted their firm's name first. I hardly ever missed a partners meeting, but critically I was on holiday in Majorca with my family when the subject came up. It was possibly a deal-breaker and to cut the Gordian knot it was agreed to have two names. They would be Pumfreys & Stonehams for clients that came from the Pumfreys side and Stonehams & Pumfreys for those that came from the Stonehams side. New clients could be allocated at random. I suspect that I do not need to record the chaos that ensued. Secretaries, particularly temps, regularly used the wrong notepaper. Answering the telephone required both names to be used and when appearing in court one had to be careful to use the correct name as otherwise the judge would say "But we have a different name here", pointing to his papers. I like to think, if I had been at the original partners meeting, I would have persuaded my other partners to have one name only, but the interesting question then arises as to whether the merger would have actually gone ahead.

After the two firms had joined up the senior partner of Stoneham & Sons told me a story of a merger between two law firms where everything was thought to have been agreed. The name of the new firm however was never discussed because each senior partner assumed his firm's name would come first. To celebrate the merger there was a grand party of the partners and staff of both firms. At an appropriate point one senior partner got up and gave a toast to "Smith & Brown." The other then stood up and said "My friend is mistaken, here's to Brown & Smith." At this point the party came to a sudden end and the merger never did take place. I have often since wondered whether my new partner was Mr Smith or Mr Brown.

Sometime later – it was well over a year if I recall things correctly – common sense at last prevailed and Pumfreys & Stonehams went forever and the new firm became known only as Stonehams & Pumfreys. All the partners had by now realised that the Stonehams name was known internationally and sensibly had to come first. A foreign lawyer when consulting a law directory and looking for Stonehams would very likely miss us if our firm name was shown in the directory as Pumfreys & Stonehams. It simply made no sense to lose potential business for the sake of a particular name.

Although I had already been involved in almost every type of litigation there was I now had the opportunity to take part in many more international cases which was something that I was particularly interested in. This led on to other ventures as I shall describe in due course.

CHAPTER THREE

Criminal Law

In or about 1970 my firm had to move offices. Developers were tearing down our nice old building and putting up a modern structure instead. I was sad to leave Clements Inn because, despite the regular rendition of "Oranges and Lemons" on the bells of St. Clement Danes which cut through the air like a knife, it was a quiet place to work; it was also of course a very convenient location for a litigator as I could get to any court in The Royal Courts of Justice within about five minutes.

At the time it was difficult to find office space in London and virtually all the partners were engaged in looking at potential sites. Eventually I saw a suite of offices in Great Marlborough Street and, although it was in no way ideal, we took a lease and moved in to what was somewhat cramped accommodation. The offices were conveniently almost next door to Great Marlborough Street magistrates court and I appeared there as an advocate on a number of occasions.

From the beginning I always did some criminal work but, because our branch offices at one time had nobody with such expertise, I had a run of about 10 years when I acted for a large number of clients accused of a variety of criminal offences. I suppose though my first criminal case, although I was only an observer, was that of Mrs Christofi whose trial at the Old Bailey I attended when I was still a student at university. Mrs Christofi, an illiterate Greek Cypriot woman, was charged with murdering her daughter in law, a German girl called Hella, by battering her, strangling her and then burning the body in the garden of Hella's home in South Hill Park, Hampstead. Mrs Christofi was very jealous of her daughter in law and may have been insane although this was not part of her defence.

The day I attended the trial was the day when the forensic scientists gave their evidence. I recall that one of them produced a bloodstained shoe which he kept in a large glass jar tightly sealed with a lid. On being examined by the prosecution, he unscrewed the lid by twisting it a number of times. "There is blood here, here and here" he said pointing to different parts of the shoe. Being a meticulous scientist he then put the shoe back in the jar and screwed the lid tight. The defence counsel then cross examined. "I should like you to show us again the blood on the heel" he said. The scientist wrestled with the jar. He had closed it too tight. He even had to put the jar between his legs. Finally the scientist got the jar open and was able to respond to the questions put to him. Having answered all the questions, the scientist put the shoe away and sealed the jar.

The prosecution counsel now decided to re-examine. "If we may look at the shoe once again" he said. I now felt sorry for the scientist who again had over tightened the lid. This time it took even more effort to get the lid off. It is strange how odd things like this stick in the memory whereas the significance of the blood on the shoe has escaped me. I also recall that I was sitting not far away from Mrs Christofi's son and I did wonder what thoughts were going through that poor man's head. It later appeared that Mrs Christofi was not unused to murder trials as when she was living in Cyprus she was tried for murdering her mother in law by ramming a burning torch down her throat. On that occasion Mrs Christofi was acquitted. This time however Mrs Christofi was not so lucky and she was convicted of murder and sentenced to death. Mrs Christofi then met the hangman in December 1954.

The next - and indeed the last - woman to be hanged was Ruth Ellis who amazingly also committed her crime in South Hill Park (what are the odds on that?). Ruth Ellis, as older readers may recall, shot her lover, one David Blakely, in the street just outside the Magdala Tavern. Ruth Ellis fired six shots, one of which missed and ricocheted off the pavement, then off the pub wall and finally struck the thumb of a lady who was passing by. There was when I last visited the area a plaque on the wall of the pub to show where the bullets had struck. Ruth Ellis was convicted and sentenced to death. Many members of the public were appalled and some 50,000 people signed a petition for clemency, but the Home Secretary was obdurate. Ruth Ellis was then hanged in July 1955.

Hangings for murder continued and the last man to be hanged was on 13 August 1964. Hangings were then suspended for five years in 1965 and finally abolished in 1969. I personally never agreed with the death sentence, not so much because it was morally wrong (although I did feel that it was), but rather that mistakes can be made and hanging an innocent person is one mistake that cannot be undone.

One of the questions non-lawyers regularly ask lawyers is how can you act for someone that you know to be guilty? The key word in this question is "know". Generally a client accused of a criminal offence will provide some explanation which indicates that he is innocent of the charge. The explanation may depend on facts that are far-fetched, but odd things do happen in life and it is the lawyer's job to defend the client to the best of his ability - and certainly irrespective of any doubts he may have as to his client's innocence.

Doctor Johnson put it well, as Boswell related in "The Journal of a Tour to the Hebrides" in stating that "A lawyer has no business with the justice or injustice of the cause which he undertakes, unless his client asks his opinion, and then he is bound to give it honestly. The justice or injustice of the cause is to be decided by the judge." It is of course a different situation when the client admits that he is guilty of the offence and you have no reason to believe it to be a false confession. Then it would be quite improper for the lawyer to put forward a case inconsistent with what his client has told him. However it would still be perfectly proper to plead not guilty and ask the State to prove its case.

There is a story I have heard (which I hope is apocryphal) that a client went to see a solicitor and told him that he had been charged with a serious criminal offence. "You must tell me exactly what happened" said the solicitor. "It was like this" said the client who went on to explain why he was not guilty. "The jury will never accept that unlikely story" said the solicitor "so please tell me now what really happened." The client thought for a few moments and then gave a new explanation. "No," said the solicitor "that preposterous tale will never persuade a jury, so please stop telling me tales and give me the true facts." The client took a little longer this time before he replied. Eventually the client said "It was like this" and he gave a third version. "Ah," said the solicitor "I believe that the jury might accept that account and now you have told me the truth I can represent you."

A case which shows how pleading not guilty can work to the client's advantage when the odds are stacked against him is that of a client who I shall call Mr Morris. Mr Morris was charged with careless driving. He and three friends were driving through Hampstead intending to go towards central London. At the tube station instead of turning down hill as they should have done Mr Morris drove up Holly Hill which is a very narrow road with a high wall on the left and on that day parked cars on the right. It was getting dark, but Mr Morris' car lights were not on and the street lighting was not good. Mr Morris's car hit the first parked car, bounced off the

41

wall and then proceeded to write off or damage two more parked cars.

Mr Morris instructed me to act for him and I advised him that he could plead guilty when he would probably get a low fine or plead not guilty which would likely attract a larger fine if he was convicted. On the facts I was given I advised that it would be best for Mr Morris to plead guilty. Mr Morris however said that it was the poor street lighting that was the cause of the accident and he insisted on pleading not guilty.

I duly turned up at Hampstead magistrates court where the case was listed to be heard by a bench of three lay magistrates. The owners of the parked cars gave evidence of hearing loud bangs, looking out of their windows and being horrified to see their cars being smashed up. A police officer then gave evidence of arriving at the scene, interviewing the four young men and noting the damage to the parked cars. He also described the length of the skid marks (indicating the speed of the vehicle). I asked some questions of the officer about the quality of the street lights and suggested to him that they were insufficiently bright. No other evidence was called and the prosecution closed its case.

I could not believe my luck. I stood up and said that I was not calling any evidence and that I would ask for the charge to be dismissed. I can recall now one of the wing magistrates - a lady - turning to the male chairman and saying "What's he talking about?" I gave her the answer. "The reason for my application" I said "is that nobody has identified my client as the driver of the car." This was indeed the case. The police had slipped up. I suspect that the magistrates had every reason to believe that my client was driving the car, but they could do nothing about it other than dismiss the charge. The State had failed to prove its case. I know that some readers will say that this is another case where a lawyer got his client off on a technicality, as if that was somehow wrong. However the law requires - and in my view properly requires - the State to prove its case. It is not for the accused to prove his innocence.

A case which exemplifies that it is up to the judge - or the jury in many cases - to decide upon guilt is that of another client whom I shall call Mr Green. Mr Green was charged with growing cannabis in his garden. This was as it turned out factually correct, but our defence was that Mr Green was unaware of the nature of the plant. Mr Green told me what had occurred and that was the defence we put forward.

Mr Green said that he had bought his house not long before and that the previous owners had cleared out their belongings quite efficiently. However they did leave behind in a chest of drawers a seed packet with some seeds in it, but unlabelled. Mr Green decided that he would plant the seeds to see what would come up. In due course some green plants emerged, but Mr Green did not know what they were.

One day Mr Green came home to see a note attached to his plants asking him to attend at the police station. The police asked Mr Green about the plants and he admitted that he was the one who planted them; the police then asked Mr Green what he did for a living and he told them that he was a landscape gardener!

Mr Green had not consulted any encyclopedia of plants (surprisingly) but nevertheless I wanted to find out if he had sown the seeds in the least favourable place as if so it might indicate that he did not know what he was planting. I therefore sent my articled clerk to Camden Market and he duly returned with a book called "How to Grow the Best Grass." As far as I can remember the book suggested that under a window ledge against a wall would be ideal place to grow cannabis. Unfortunately for me this was exactly where the plants were.

Undaunted I flung the book into the nearest waste paper basket.

I prepared the defence brief and instructed a barrister to represent Mr Green in court. I also sent an articled clerk to court to take notes and look after the client. I fully realised that we were likely to have an uphill battle. The articled clerk arrived back from court at about 6 p.m. I must admit that I was not optimistic. "How did it go?" I asked him. "Mr Green was acquitted" he said gleefully. The jury had believed my client - and who is to say they were not right.

One of the occasions when I appeared in Great Marlborough Street magistrates court was when I represented my au pair. The au pair had taken a necklace from a stand at Selfridges and then proceeded to leave the store with the necklace in her hands. The charge of theft came up at Great Marlborough Street magistrates court as did all cases of shoplifting at stores in that part of the West End. This was a problem because it was likely that the magistrates who were sitting would have sat on so many shoplifting charges that they would have already heard every possible explanation for suspicious behaviour.

My au pair's defence was that she was in a state of automatism at the time and was completely unaware that she was walking to the exit with a necklace in her hands. I am sorry to say that my advocacy was unsuccessful on this occasion and that my au pair was duly convicted and fined. I was though successful on another occasion at the same court when I was also acting for a client accused of shoplifting After the case I recall saying to the store detective "I trust there are no hard feelings" to which she replied "Yes there are" as she strode off in a huff.

A case where I acted for another of my au pairs was heard at Highgate magistrates court immediately after Christmas one year. I recall that it was a day when the office was shut and I drove to the court from my home. I was not pleased on more than one count. My au pair told me that she had gone into the changing room in a shop in Golders Green just before Christmas and had stuck a pair of trousers up her sweater. As the au pair was quite busty any way it must not have been too difficult for the shop assistant to conclude that something was not quite right. In any event the au pair was stopped, searched and arrested.

When the case was called I told the magistrates that my client was pleading guilty, but wanted the following facts taken into consideration. I said that the young lady was away from her home in France and her friends there and, having little income, was envious of the wealthy shoppers that were spending a lot of money on Christmas presents. I said that my client had eventually succumbed to temptation. The chairman of the magistrates then interrupted and said somewhat unfairly I believe "Do you know who the employer of this young lady is who does not pay her a proper weekly wage?" I wished that I could have been somewhere else. "I am" I said somewhat sheepishly. I doubt that this admission helped my advocacy, but fortunately the au pair was only fined £15, which just happened to be the cost of the trousers in question.

Another recollection involving an au pair made me very aware that coincidences can occur in real life which, if described in a work of fiction, would be regarded as too far-fetched. One day I was due to fly to Paris to see a client and, as I expected to be back in time, I agreed to play in an evening match as part of a badminton team. I can recall advising the client over a splendid lunch in the open air near the Arc de Triomphe and then catching an early flight back.

In those days there was a terminal in Gloucester Road linked by coach to Heathrow. On arriving at Heathrow I accordingly took the coach and arrived at the terminal in the late afternoon. I left the building and hailed a taxi which pulled out into Cromwell Road and stopped at the traffic lights which were red. There was another taxi alongside. The driver of the other taxi leant out and said to my taxi driver "Do you know where Heath View is mate?" in a cockney accent. Now it so happened that this was the very road in East Finchley where I lived, although I had asked my taxi driver to take me to East Finchley station where I had left my car. I then recalled that my wife was getting a new au pair that day from Austria called Ingrid and, seeing that there was a young lady with blonde hair in the back of the other taxi, I thought this could be her. "Can you ask your fare if she is Ingrid?" I said. Without querying this strange request the taxi driver looked over his shoulder and said "Are you Ingrid, love?" The answer was no. I persevered. "Ask her if she comes from Austria?" I said. The answer was again no. Without really considering what impact my actions would have on the young lady I told the taxi driver that I could show him the way to Heath View and I jumped into the back of his taxi. The blonde passenger, not surprisingly, looked taken aback so I thought I must quickly assure her that I was not some predator. Possibly because I had just come from France and possibly because she looked as if she could be French I said "Bonjour mademoiselle, quelle maison en Heath View visitez vous?" "Quarante" she replied. That just happened to be the number of my house, so I explained to the young lady that I was her new employer. What she made of meeting me in such a way I never found out. As though she decided to stay for only three days perhaps she thought that I was a practitioner in the black arts.

When I arrived home I was in a hurry to get to my badminton match in time so I quickly introduced Monique (which was in fact her name) to my bemused wife and I shot off, leaving my wife to fathom out how on earth the two of us could have met up. I later found out that what had actually happened was that Ingrid from Austria had a last minute change of mind and the agency had replaced her with Monique from Nice, who had been waiting for a family to take her on as an au pair and was prepared to come on short notice.

One of the more significant criminal trials I was involved in concerned four brothers who were charged with kidnapping and assault. They were alleged to have been involved in a gang fight and three of the brothers were believed to have kidnapped a member of the other gang in revenge for a near fatal attack on their younger brother. The victim's case was that he was bundled into a car and taken somewhere where he was tortured by having hot water poured over him, by having his bare feet stamped on by heavy boots and by being hit on the head with some sort of hammer. The victim then said that the three brothers told him they were going to dump him in a nearby pit, but on the way they stopped at his house and bundled him out of the car.

The trial took place at the Old Bailey and I instructed an excellent young barrister called Michael Kennedy to appear for the alleged kidnappers. The prosecution laid out its case and then called the victim to give his evidence of the dramatic experience he had suffered. Michael Kennedy then rose to cross examine and he asked him what on returning home did he say to his grandfather who was asleep in the house. "I did not say anything because he is an old man and I did not want to wake him up" was the reply. The victim also admitted that he never went to hospital or consulted a doctor. After a six weeks hearing the three elder brothers were acquitted. The younger brother who was charged with assault never turned up for trial and I believe went to Australia. There were a number of other defendants who were involved in the fighting but they were all convicted.

In the community in which the brothers lived my firm I believe achieved the reputation of being hot criminal lawyers, as I suspect it was believed - wrongly I hasten to add - that we had advised the three elder brothers to stand trial and had advised the younger one to disappear. In fact the younger brother did return to England later and was convicted of assault and received, if I recall correctly, a lenient sentence.

Another trial I had at the Old Bailey involved a young man who was charged with selling prohibited drugs in a club in the West End. The defendant wanted the best possible representation and I therefore briefed Frederick Elwyn Jones Q.C. who had prosecuted at the Nuremburg war trials and was later to become Lord Chancellor. It would be difficult to find a more charming and kindly person who was also such a significant legal figure.

I can recall one day my secretary rushing over to the Old Bailey with some documents. When she arrived Frederick Elwyn Jones suggested that we discussed something over a bite of lunch. My secretary tactfully retreated, but Frederick Elwyn Jones said "And you too, my dear." Such a courtesy was unusual in a Q.C. in those days.

All I can now remember of that case is that I asked my client to dress in such a fashion that he did not look like a drug trafficker. I do not actually know if my client took my advice or not, but he dressed in an all black outfit and had on tinted glasses and I regret to say was in due course convicted.

Most of my more significant criminal cases were heard in London, but on one occasion I recall having a trial at Lewes in Sussex. The case concerned a young conservatives' dance in a farmer's barn near Billingshurst in Sussex. Everything was going well until some lads who may or may not have been of the same political persuasion gate-crashed the party. Unfortunately this latter group drank too much and started throwing beer glasses around. At this point the young conservatives thought it wise to beat a quick retreat and they made for the farmhouse. The by this time unruly mob ran after the young men and women and the pursued dancers had in effect to barricade themselves in. One of the mob, whom I suspect had seen a film such as "Ivanhoe", picked up a thick plank of wood and with his mates tried to ram the farmhouse door. Meanwhile the irate farmer rang the police and a number of police officers then turned up and made arrests.

My client, who was not part of the unruly mob and I believe not a young conservative either, was arrested for being in the vicinity of "the battle" whilst carrying an offensive weapon, namely a heavy spanner. This, my client claimed, was for carrying out repairs to his car which was unreliable. In due course my client stood trial and was eventually acquitted. The case remains in my memory, though, not because of our success but because of two exchanges during cross examination. First one should know that just before the trial the labour party had had a landslide victory at the general election. One of the young conservatives was giving evidence that he was one of the last to run from the barn and that when he got to the farmhouse door it was being shut, but he was just able to squeeze through. "That's one conservative that got in then" said the judge dryly. The young conservative guarding the farmhouse door then gave evidence and he explained that the door was only slightly open. The barrister cross examining asked how wide the gap was. "Exactly one foot" was his reply. "How can you be so precise?" said the barrister. "Because it was my foot that was in it" was the unexpected response.

A slightly unusual, albeit frustrating, case where I was the advocate took place in Bromley magistrates court. The client was charged with a criminal assault on his wife which supposedly occurred in the high street of a nearby town. The wife, not surprisingly, was the chief prosecution witness. I stood to cross examine. "I put it to you" I said "that this assault never took place at all and that you have made it all up." "No," said the woman "it is just like the last occasion when he hit me." This was an unfortunate reply, because no charges had ever been made against my client with regard to any previous assault and mention of it might well prejudice the magistrates against him. I therefore asked the magistrates for the case to be stopped and listed before a different bench. The magistrates agreed and asked us to wait because another bench of magistrates were sitting in a different court and were expected to finish their case early. I asked the magistrates to request the probation officer to tell the wife that she was not allowed to mention the earlier alleged assault and this they did.

My client and I waited patiently and not long afterwards we were called back into the other court. I got to the same point in my cross examination and got exactly the same reply. The client however was keen to press on, so I simply asked the magistrates to disregard the wife's reply. The doctor who examined the wife then gave evidence of the bruising that he had observed. "Is the bruising" I asked "of such a nature that it is as consistent with self-infliction as it is of an assault?" "I would not say that" said the doctor and my hopes were temporarily dashed. "It is" he said " in fact more consistent with self-infliction." My hopes soared and rightly so as my client was duly acquitted.

An unusual case in some respects was that of a client I shall call Miss Trainer. Miss Trainer was charged with receiving stolen property. Miss Trainer lived on her own and

50

taught at a nearby school. One day a parcel arrived addressed to her and she opened it and found some items, let us say sweaters. However there was no indication of where they had come from. The next week another parcel and so on. Miss Trainer received wine, cigarettes and gardening tools (despite having no garden). At one point Miss Trainer went to the post office and said that the parcels were not for her, but she was told that if they were addressed to her they were hers. Unfortunately the police took a different view and Miss Trainer was prosecuted.

The case went to trial and we put forward the defence that Miss Trainer did not know and had no reasonable basis for knowing that the goods were stolen. Fortunately for Miss Trainer she was acquitted. After the case I discovered what the police had suspected. Parcels sent by post when carried by rail sometimes came undone. In that situation the parcels were sent to a particular location (near Rugby I think) where a team of postal officials would re-parcel and re-label. However dishonest employees discovered that it was not that difficult to re-address the parcels to friends and later share the contents. The police had believed that Miss Trainer was just such a friend. Miss Trainer herself believed that the parents of one of the children she taught at school and may have been thought to have favoured were giving her a number of rewards. If that was in fact the case the gifts were certainly poisoned chalices. As far as I know the identity of the sender was never discovered, but to Miss Trainer's relief the parcels stopped coming after the court case had taken place.

One of the clients I acted for quite early in my career was charged with burglary. The client had a string of convictions for housebreaking, theft and suchlike. It was vital that the jury did not know of this as it would very likely prejudice their minds against him. In those days the rule was that the jury were not entitled to know of previous convictions, but there were exceptions. One was that if a police witness was accused by the defence of lying the State could then give evidence of the defendant's criminal record.

I had instructed a particular barrister at the express request of my senior partner who had met him socially. Unfortunately the barrister was a pompous man who thought he knew more that he actually did. During cross examination of a police witness the barrister said "I put it to you that you are mistaken" "No" said the officer. "I put it to you that your memory is at fault." "No" said the officer. "I put it to you that you are ly…" I quickly grabbed the barrister's gown and said "You can't say that because if you do his record will go in." The barrister brushed me aside and said "I know what I am doing." Turning back to the witness he completed his sentence. "I put it to you that you are lying." "No I am not" said the officer. Accordingly nothing had been gained and, as I at the time suspected, everything had been lost. The client's record was later read out to the jury and they not perhaps surprisingly convicted him and the judge gave him a sentence of four years.

After a conviction it is customary for the solicitor and the barrister to visit the client in the cells and discuss with him whether there is a reasonable chance of an appeal against conviction and/or sentence. Mr Pompous Barrister was however nowhere to be seen so I went down to the cells alone. I told my client that I was very sorry that he had got four years, but he took it all in his stride and said "Never mind you got me a great barrister - did you see the way he had a go at that police officer." I felt in all the circumstances that it would not help matters to tell him that that was likely to be the main reason why the jury had decided to find him guilty.

Having described one unlikeable barrister I should put the record straight and say that some of the most charming barristers I met were at the criminal bar. Two I briefed regularly were Reggie Batt and Michael Kennedy. Michael, who was the barrister in my kidnapping case, went on to be a judge, but Reggie died prematurely young. Reggie was for me a slimmed down version of Rumpole of the Bailey.

When I first met Reggie Batt he could not drive and I can remember one occasion where we acted for a lady charged with dangerous driving. Reggie got an acquittal and after the case he and I accepted a lift from our client back to the railway station. It was not a long journey, but it was truly hair raising. The lady swerved all over the road, went through traffic lights as they were turning red and overtook in dangerous places. We were both white faced when we left the car. It is perhaps the only case in my career where I later wished we had lost it.

Later Reggie got a car and I remember one case where I met him at court. He looked a little flustered and I asked him what was wrong. Reggie told me that as he was parking he had accidentally struck and damaged the judge's car. "Do you think I should tell him now?" he asked me. "No" I said "Tell him after the case; if you tell him now he might not be able to sit on our case because if we lose he might think we believe that he is punishing you and if we win he might think we believe that he is leaning over backwards not to be seen to be punishing you. Reggie took my advice, but I do not recall ever discovering what the judge did say when Reggie later owned up.

In cases today where it is alleged that a motorist's driving is adversely affected by alcohol scientific methods can answer the question. When I was a young lawyer though a doctor had to put the motorist through a series of specific tests and then give evidence of how the motorist had fared. In one case my client was charged with such an offence and when the case came to trial the doctor who saw him was called to the witness stand. The doctor's evidence was that he had put the defendant through the usual series of tests, all of which he had failed. "I believe you did the matches test" said the barrister I had instructed. "Yes" said the doctor. "Please give us a demonstration" said the barrister. The doctor then dropped all the matches from a matchbox on the floor and attempted to pick them up. Whether the doctor was nervous or stiff I do not know, but he did not make a good job of this task. "And I understand you asked some mental arithmetic questions" said the barrister. "Yes" said the doctor "What is 7 x 14?" said the barrister. "96" said the doctor "or is it 88?" "And did you ask him to walk along a straight line?" "Yes" said the doctor. A line was then drawn on the court floor and the doctor walked unsteadily along it. This all took place I should explain just after the lunch break. "Have you been drinking over lunch?" said the barrister. "Certainly not" said the doctor. "Then I suggest" said the barrister looking at the jury "that on the basis of your tests you cannot be sure that my client had been drinking either." This surely deserved an acquittal, but unfortunately the jury did not agree on their verdict and the judge directed a retrial. The doctor in the meantime must have done some practising and at the retrial he was able to perform very well on all of the tests. My client was unfortunately, and I believe wrongly, convicted.

The above recollection reminds me of the story of the man charged with causing criminal damage. What do you have to say for yourself?" said the judge. "It wasn't really my fault" said the defendant "I was as drunk as a judge at the time." "You have that wrong" said the judge "It's as sober as a judge and as drunk as a lord." "Yes, my lord" said the defendant!

Another story which pokes fun at lawyers is about the Pope dying and going to Heaven. The Pope expects a grand welcome, but everything is low key. St. Peter greets him and gives him the key to his room. On his way there he hears cheering and he sees that a crowd has assembled. A man seated on cushions and surrounded by drapes is being carried on a palanquin to his quarters, whilst the people around cheer and cheer. The Pope turns to St. Peter and says "Who is that?" That is a solicitor" says St. Peter. "I don't understand "says the Pope "I represent God on earth and yet I had no such welcome." "Ah" said St Peter "that is true, but we have had many popes and this is one of the very few solicitors to make it."

The Americans have a similar attitude to lawyers. My favourite American anti-lawyer joke is "What is the difference between a dead lawyer lying in the road and a dead skunk?" to which the answer is "There are skid marks in front of the skunk." Lawyers will never be the most popular profession.

In the course of representing persons charged with criminal offences I have visited various prisons. Brixton was a holding prison where people who have been charged with a criminal offence but refused bail were kept and is the one that I went to most. I believe that because the prisoners were there for comparatively short periods no real rapport was built up between prisoner and prison officer - in any event in my experience the occupants were treated with very little respect. I believed that until conviction a prisoner should be addressed as Mr Smith rather than Prisoner 583 as was the case. This seemed to me quite wrong and I have often wondered how I would be treated and how I would feel if I had suffered the misfortune to be charged with a criminal offence and refused bail.

Sometimes I interviewed clients in police cells. This was not particularly pleasant because one would be locked in the cell with the prisoner and would have to "holler" at the end of the interview to be let out. The police, who did not generally like solicitors that much, would take their time and if one happened to suffer from claustrophobia, which to a mild extent I do, it was not an enjoyable experience. When I first qualified I had finished an interview in a cell and as on this occasion the cell door was open I started to leave. A police officer said "Where are you going?" I replied that I was a solicitor who had been interviewing his client. "That's what they all say" he replied and he asked me to return to the cell. I turned around intending to ask him how many prisoners happened to carry black briefcases, but his colleagues were laughing and I realised it was just their little joke.

Criminal lawyers are an important part of the legal system. Anybody at all, however law abiding, could find themselves in certain circumstances accused of a criminal offence and possibly a serious one. At that point the innocent citizen would want - and fortunately can get in the United Kingdom - first class legal assistance. It is accordingly, in my view, regrettable that those practising in the field of criminal law are so often criticised by the public for getting the guilty off. As William Blackstone said as long ago as the eighteenth century: "It is better that ten guilty persons escape than one innocent suffer."

CHAPTER FOUR

Family law

One area of litigation that throughout my career I was regularly involved with was divorce (including custody battles and matrimonial property disputes), now generally called family law. Until 1 January 1971 when the laws of divorce were completely overhauled, the grounds of divorce were based on adultery, cruelty, desertion and insanity as I mentioned earlier when describing "Splitto." Previous to 1971 whether the marriage had broken down or not was irrelevant. This could cause great hardship to both husbands and wives who found themselves trapped in a loveless marriage. Fortunately the situation was much alleviated by the new legislation. The change in the law allowed divorces if there was an irretrievable breakdown of the marriage and the spouse bringing the case, namely the petitioner, could show adultery, unreasonable behaviour, two years desertion, two years separation with the other spouse consenting to the divorce or five years separation whether the other spouse consented or not.

In the mid-sixties when reform of the divorce laws was being widely debated various schemes were put forward. One was a proposal by none other than Sir Jocelyn Simon, the Head of the Probate, Divorce and Admiralty Division of the High Court - known by lawyers as "wills, wives and wrecks." Sir Jocelyn suggested that spouses with children under 17 should not be allowed to divorce at all. I thought that this was such a bad idea that I was spurred into writing a letter to "The Times." Sir Jocelyn was concerned that unless there was some such restriction there would be more broken homes. I pointed out in my letter that adulterous spouses often leave the home to go off with the other man or woman, that the cruel conduct of one spouse often drives the other from the house and that desertion by definition means that cohabitation has come to an end. I then suggested that where, for financial reasons or otherwise, the parties still lived in the same house the home could be just as broken. I then wrote "If divorce, which is after all principally the right to remarry, were forbidden to couples with children under 17, I think that rather than fewer broken homes there would be more illicit unions... and a rise in the illegitimacy rate." I also pointed out the injustice to spouses with young children in comparison to their childless counterparts. Looking back to that time it is interesting to note the substantial shift that has occurred in social values. Nobody today really talks of illicit unions and nowadays it is quite common for young people to live together before marriage, if indeed a marriage ever follows. In the mid-sixties it was a somewhat different story. In any event Sir Jocelyn's views did not prompt any change in the law.

Acting for divorce clients in my view required special human skills as well as a detailed knowledge of law and procedure. The ability to listen intently to the client and look sympathetic was a must. This was not really difficult for me as most of the time I was indeed fully sympathetic to the client's plight. If not I just had to pretend. Further I firmly believed that it was absolutely vital that interviews were not interrupted by telephone calls or indeed anything else. It was important, especially for this type of client, that he or she felt that they had your full attention. I always told my secretary that, unless there was a fire, I was not to be disturbed. Being, or pretending to be, sympathetic though did not of course mean that I should only tell clients what they wanted to hear. It was also important to be absolutely straight with the client and to give clear and firm advice.

Occasionally some clients would want to "play dirty" and when I said I would not go along with any dishonest or unprofessional tactics they would move on to another solicitor. Such clients often "went through" a number of solicitors. I recall one male client who having already sacked about five previous solicitors left me for this reason. I later read that the solicitor that he went to was struck off the roll of solicitors - presumably for some form of misconduct. What happened to my once client though I did not discover. I should add that making tactical moves was perfectly acceptable but there was in my view a clear line, however difficult to define, which should never be crossed.

When I saw clients - and this was particularly so for divorce clients - I used to remove all other files from my desk. The idea was to give the client the impression (which also happened to be the reality) that I was concentrating on their case only. This however backfired one day when a client prolonged the interview and said that I would not mind because I was clearly not very busy as I had no other files on my desk. Nevertheless I preferred my approach to having a high pile of files in full view. In this context I recall going to see another solicitor at the beginning of my career. I was ushered into his office. There was a large pile of files on the solicitor's desk, but he was nowhere to be seen. I waited patiently. After about one or two minutes a voice came from behind the files and a gentleman of somewhat short stature emerged and introduced himself. In those early days Dickens did not seem long dead!

My philosophy in handling divorce cases was as far as possible not to vilify the other spouse - particularly where there were children. This was sometimes difficult to achieve as clients in the throes of a divorce could become very bitter.

I recollect one case where the husband came home one evening and found a note for him from his wife with a list headed "Ten things I hate about you." The husband sadly took part in this exercise and penned a reply headed "Ten things I hate about you too."

I also recall cases where there were acrimonious disputes over possessions. Instead of fighting things out in court I would recommend that the parties listed everything they owned jointly or separately and then tossed a coin. The winner would have first choice and could choose one item, selecting by value or by sentiment. The other spouse would then have their turn and so on. The usual response was something like "But what happens if my husband wins and chooses the antique desk I bought at Sotheby's." Looking back now I am not sure if my suggestion was ever taken up. Of course the upside of my suggestion being rejected was that my firm made a lot more money out of the dispute than they would have done otherwise. I did though really try to save my clients from using up their resources on legal costs wherever I could.

Two techniques which I used in divorce cases which I have not seen described elsewhere were "the magic wand" and "win a jaguar". The first technique is to tell the client that he or she has a magic wand and can have what they like, but only one wish. Sometimes the answer was illuminating and very different from the client's original instructions - often because the client did not think such an objective possible. The second technique is to tell the client that he or she must place their objectives in the correct order of importance to win a jaguar. Again the results can be illuminating. For example a client might say "custody, capital, maintenance and divorce" which would generally require the case to be run in quite a different way to that if the objectives had been in the reverse order.

One oddity, as it now seems to me, was that prior to the changes in the law the petitioner had to be asked by their solicitor if they needed to make a discretion statement. "What do you mean?" was the usual response and I had to explain to clients that if they had themselves committed adultery they had to give full details in a discretion statement. These details had to include the name of the other person and the dates when adultery occurred - and it had to be updated if the adultery continued. Indeed it was my normal advice to tell clients to stop adultery forthwith and wait for the decree absolute. You can imagine how well this advice went down when the client had started a new and possibly permanent relationship. When the case came to court the judge, where there was a discretion statement, had the right to refuse a decree even if the grounds for divorce were fully made out. Accordingly, even in cases where both spouses had found new partners, there was a danger that the judge would direct that they remained married to each other. "What a nonsense" you might say and I would certainly agree. There was also a State official called the Queen's Proctor whose job it was to check up on divorce cases to see if there had been collusion between the parties or if the court had in any way been misled or deceived. One aspect of this job was accordingly to see that anybody who had committed adultery did not obtain a divorce unless they had disclosed it and asked in effect for forgiveness. A sorry state of affairs that truly was, but now fortunately behind us.

On the subject of discretion statements I remember one occasion when a very young lady client blushed when I asked her if she needed to make a discretion statement. She said that she did and I gave her some paper and asked her to write down the details. Meanwhile I looked at other documents in the file. The lady wrote furiously and then looked up and asked for more paper. In the end we filed one of the longest discretion statements I was ever involved with. On another occasion one of my partners told me that he had told a male client that he must confess to any adultery that he had committed. The client said that he did not need to make any discretion statement as he had not committed any adultery.

61

Later, after the client had obtained his decree absolute, he said to my partner "I am right aren't I in that I did not have to disclose my having intercourse during day time." I suspect that the client thought adultery was like burglary and could only be committed at night.

Adultery had to be strictly proved and it was not uncommon where both parties wanted a divorce for the man to go to Brighton or Eastbourne with a lady from an escort agency who would climb into his bed just before the waitress arrived with the morning breakfast. The waitress would then give evidence and the court would assume in such a situation that sexual intercourse had taken place. The court was being deceived and the judge probably knew it. Of course there may also have been occasions where the lady in fact succumbed to the charms of her companion. An alternative was for the man to make a written confession of his infidelity, but this was originally viewed with some scepticism and there was no guarantee that the judge would accept it as true. Confession statements were usually effective though when taken from the third party - usually the man who admitted to sleeping with the wife (known as the co-respondent). Such men were often cooperative because on many occasions the liaison was continuing and the co-respondent wanted the husband to obtain a divorce so that he could marry his wife. The downside though was that signing the confession statement would quite likely mean that the co-respondent had to pay the costs of the divorce. I suspect that on some occasions this was too high a burden for the philanderer and the unfortunate wife was then abandoned by both men.

Diverting for a moment I once dictated a bill of costs to a new secretary. One aspect of every bill in those days was to state that one had read the letters that the client and others had sent to the firm. However to make it seem more weighty it was the almost universal custom to state that one had "perused the correspondence." The bill in question was to a divorce client and after reciting the various steps I had taken it ended with "and finally pursuing the co-respondents." Fortunately I spotted the mistake and corrected the bill before it went out.

Returning to confession statements I recall being in court when one of my partners had to give evidence of having taken down a confession statement. My partner gave his evidence and read from the statement which he had in his hand. The judge had his own copy, but decided that he wanted to see the original. My partner handed the document to the usher who in the course of handing it to the judge happened to turn the document over. "But this is not a confession statement" said the judge "It seems to be a draft of a land transfer." Unfortunately when writing down the confession statement my partner had grabbed the nearest bit of paper to hand and had not then realised that there was anything on the reverse side until after the man making the confession had left. My partner had hoped that as the judge had his own copy nobody would ever know. In the end my partner got a lecture from the judge along the lines that economies were broadly worthy but not to this extent.

In adultery cases, if the man was not prepared to take a trip to the seaside and nobody was prepared to make a written confession, matters were not then straightforward. Some evidence of opportunity and desire that was compelling was required. In this connection I recollect acting for a lady who wanted her husband to divorce her as she had no grounds for divorcing him. The lady had formed a new relationship with an American gentleman who happened to be a professional photographer. The boyfriend suggested that, although he would rather not, he was prepared to fix a camera to the end of the bed and take photos of the wife and himself making love which he would then post to me. I hastily turned this offer down - apart from anything else I did not want to be prosecuted for receiving pornographic photographs through the post. Fortunately in the end we were able to provide other evidence of the adultery, the husband got his divorce and I hope that the wife and her American boyfriend had a long and happy marriage.

I acted in divorce cases for almost seven years before I myself got married. Not being married did not in fact cause me any problems in acting for my divorce clients, but I do recall one case where a female client was explaining something quite intimate and she suddenly stopped and said "Do you understand what I am saying - are you yourself married?" "No", I said "but I have lots of experience." I meant in handling divorce cases, but by the look in her eye I think she took it the other way.

An unusual case was that of a lady I shall call Mrs Wood. Mrs Wood instructed me to represent her in a divorce case. At the time she was living separate from her husband. One day a good looking man knocked on Mrs Wood's door. The man said that he was a private detective and that her husband had instructed him to check if she was living with or associating with another man. "Come in and see for yourself" Mrs Wood answered - and the man did just that. After checking in the wardrobes and under the beds and finding no one, he went away. A few days later the man returned, but instead of asking to search the property he asked Mrs Wood out for a drink. Mrs Wood unwisely agreed and on their return Mrs Wood invited the man in for coffee and in due course they ended up in the bedroom. A short time later three men, namely the husband, the husband's father and the detective's boss, arrived at Mrs Wood's property. They broke open the front door and ran up the stairs to the bedroom where they found Mrs Wood in bed with the detective. I understand that the three men made very unflattering remarks about Mrs Wood's morals and then went away. All of this all came out in court later, but our attempts to track down the detective and call him to give evidence that it was a put up job met with no success. Of course even if we were able to obtain such evidence such would not negate the adultery, but it would likely place the husband in a bad light and to some extent balance the books. In any event we were told that the detective had emigrated to New Zealand and that indeed may have been the case. Nevertheless Mrs Wood got her divorce as far as I recall.

One family law case which was particularly interesting involved the film actress Dawn Addams She is perhaps little known now, but she was a very attractive lady who appeared in many films, including with Charlie Chaplin in "A King in New York." Miss Addams married an Italian, one Prince Massimo and became a Princess, but when I met her the couple had separated. Miss Addams had had a child with an unknown man and the press were speculating as to who the man was. I was instructed by the unknown man to obtain custody of the child and I received a number of telephone calls from newspapers asking me who the father was which I answered with no comment. One day it was decided that both parties with their solicitors should meet at Miss Addams' apartment in Belgravia to see if some agreement could be reached. As it was late in the day Miss Addams cooked us all scrambled eggs. I was a bachelor at the time and I had arranged to meet my flatmates and other friends that evening at a pub in Hampstead. I was much later than expected and I was asked where I had been. I said (truthfully) that I had been having scrambled eggs with a princess. I am sorry to say that my friends did not believe me. Perhaps they will now if they read this.

The case itself came to a very sad end. Miss Addams was appearing in the winter at a theatre in Liverpool and I believe that she took her young baby with her to rehearsals. The child unfortunately caught a cold and died. I believe that nobody at the time (except for us few) ever did find out the name of the unknown man.

Another child case I remember involved a dispute over the custody of two children. I acted for the wife whom I shall call Mrs Macdonald. Mrs Macdonald had custody but the husband who was Canadian had been given rights of access to the children. Somehow we discovered that there was a booking on a flight to Edmonton in Canada for four persons under the name Macdonald. We suspected that Mr Macdonald and his lady friend were going to take his children out of school and then onto this flight, so we obtained a court order forbidding this. I then sent a clerk to Heathrow with the court order and we alerted the airport police that we were on the way. My clerk got to the airport in time and, after he had waited for a while, he spotted a man, a woman and two children about to check in. The man gave his name as Macdonald whereupon my clerk and the airport police accosted him. All was in vain though because it turned out to be a completely different family who just happened to have the same name. Looking back I do hope that we did not spoil the Macdonald family's trip too much.

Another custody dispute comes to mind. I represented the husband in court and the wife was represented by a barrister. I had three good points to make and I addressed the judge for about five minutes, made my three points and then sat down. The barrister stood up and spoke for about twenty minutes. The judge thought for a few moments and then decided in favour of my client. As my client and I were walking away from the court I could see that he was not looking as happy as I had expected. "Are you not happy with the result?" I said. "Oh, yes" he replied "the result is great, I'm just not over happy with your performance; my wife's barrister spoke for twenty minutes, but you only spoke for five." "But we won and you have the children" I said. He was not convinced -

clearly a man more concerned with the length rather than the quality of the cloth!

I had to obtain an injunction to prevent a parent removing his child out of the country in another custody case. I was instructed very late in the day and by the time I got to the High Court all the judges had gone home. I was advised however to go a flat in the Temple which was nearby and call on a specific High Court judge who might be able to help. I found the flat and knocked on the door. The judge, who was getting ready for some formal function and was halfway through tying his bow tie answered the door. "I am sorry to trouble you my Lord" I said "but I need an injunction to stop a parent taking his child abroad against the wishes of the other parent who has custody of the child." "But you will need a barrister" the judge said in a kindly voice. I was near the beginning of my career and in the rush had forgotten that in theory we were in open court, as distinct to being in chambers, and I had no right of audience. "Why don't you go downstairs" said the judge "there's a set of chambers there and there may be a barrister who could assist, but you will have to hurry as I am going out."

I quickly ran downstairs and went into the chambers where I saw a gentleman in the course of taking out his contact lenses. I asked him if he was a barrister and, when he confirmed that he was, I asked him to represent my client in applying for an injunction. "When is the hearing?" the barrister asked. "In about two minutes time" I replied. The barrister gave me some paper and I hastily wrote up a brief on which I marked his fee as was the custom. I think from memory all it said was "Please act for the wife in a custody dispute." As we went up the stairs I told the barrister the relevant facts. The barrister knocked on the judge's door. "Good evening my Lord, I have just been instructed in this case" the barrister said. That certainly was as true a statement

67

as he ever made. The barrister continued and the judge who was now fully and formally dressed gave us our injunction. Although maybe I should have realised the need for a barrister I could not in fact have acted much quicker than I did.

The unexpected is the expected when it comes to acting in divorce cases. Once a lady who lived out of London, let us call her Mrs Richards, asked me to advise her on her matrimonial rights whilst she was still living with her husband. I had a series of interviews with her on a weekly basis. Mrs Richards was always smartly dressed. One day on her arrival she told me that her husband suspected her of seeing another man. "Who does he suspect?" I said. "You" was the answer that caught me by surprise. "Why is that?" I said. "Because" she answered "every Thursday I dress up in my best clothes and come up to town, evidently to meet somebody." I advised her that she should stop seeing me forthwith unless she had clearly made up her mind to divorce her husband. I did not in fact see her again and fortunately I was never confronted by an irate husband. I hope things got better for her.

Another case which "threw" me at the time was one where one of the most beautiful women I have ever met asked me to advise her on her matrimonial rights. The lady told me that after some years of marriage she had decided to leave her husband for somebody else. I said that I would need full details of the man in question. "It's not a him it's a her" the client explained. I suspect my surprise was writ large on my face.

In advising in matrimonial cases it is often important to consider how one's client would appear to the judge in court. In one custody dispute I advised my very well dressed lady client to wear something more homely and give the impression that she loved baking cakes. My client took my advice and turned up for court wearing something like a patterned cardigan and presenting a dramatic contrast to her husband's new wife who was dressed in a beautifully tailored black outfit with smart high heeled shoes. I was particularly pleased that in finding in our favour the judge commented on the homeliness of my client and the smartness of the new wife! This contrasted with, as previously recounted, my lack of success in the case involving drug distribution where my client wore a black outfit and had on tinted glasses. Well, you can't win them all!

Giving evidence in court, perhaps of delicate matters, can be difficult for some clients but I was only once ever worried that a client might dry up. By chance I had two divorce cases that came up for hearing on the same morning. In each case I acted for the female petitioner. One case involved my nervous client, whereas the other involved a lady who seemed to have nerves of steel and a voice to match. A barrister had been instructed to appear on behalf of the two ladies and it so happened that the stronger minded lady went first. No problem - her voice rang through the court as she described in graphic detail how her husband had mistreated her. Then the timid client. "What is your full name?" said the barrister. My client froze. The barrister tried again. My client tried to answer but the words would just not come. The lady was petrified. With a sympathetic judge progress was however made by the barrister putting the answers to his questions to my client who nodded her agreement and in this unconventional way she was able to get her divorce.

Divorce clients, because of the strong emotions often aroused, can put pressure on their solicitors. Nevertheless as I have already indicated the solicitor must resist taking any action that would be dishonest or unprofessional. I remember on one occasion agreeing with the other party's solicitor that a particular fact which we relied on was admitted and I would not have to prove it in court. However the solicitor back-tracked when we got to court. I said that we had an agreement and that he could not simply change his mind, but he responded by saying that he was acting on his client's instructions. I pointed out that he was acting on behalf of his client when he made the agreement and should not have done so if he thought it was outside his authority. The solicitor would not budge. I was absolutely furious. On the spur of the moment, though, I thought of what I believe was a pretty good put down. "You are" I said "the kind of person who believes that ethics is next to Suffolk."

On one occasion a gentleman from another country who lived abroad asked me to advise him on how he could divorce his wife who was still resident in the matrimonial home. The gentleman in question was anxious to marry a lady who lived in Britain but who was herself married. The client was unable to divorce his wife in the country where he and his wife had been living and I advised him that he could not divorce his wife in this country either. The client was however not to be thwarted and I accordingly arranged for both he and his lady friend to divorce their spouses in Mexico. I therefore instructed a Mexican lawyer who not only arranged the divorces, but also arranged the couple's wedding, the hotel accommodation, the transport and everything else. I was later told that the couple were met at the airport by a chauffeur driven car which took them to a particular hotel where they had been booked into separate rooms. These they occupied overnight. The next morning the couple were driven to the court where after two short hearings the client and his lady friend each obtained a divorce. The car was waiting and the couple were then driven to another location where they went through a ceremony of marriage. Finally the couple were driven back to their hotel where they found that all of their luggage had been moved into the bridal suite. The next morning the couple were driven back to the airport. I recall that when the bill later arrived at my offices it had one figure on it only and this was to cover all of the services provided.

Apart from this rather unusual scenario the other reason I recall this case is that I always enjoyed dictating to letters to the Mexican lawyer, particularly if I had a temp. I would start off by saying "take a letter to Whan Ernandeth, Weedath Whareth, Cheewaawaa, Mexico." I would then see if the secretary was able to work out that the letter should be addressed to Juan Hernandez, Ciudad Juarez, Chihuahua, Mexico.

Most of my divorce clients were, I believe, satisfied with the service I provided and some sufficiently so for them to give me something extra for myself despite having to pay my firm's charges which could by the nature of the job often be sizeable. I was in a way unhappy about receiving gifts but it would have been ungracious to refuse.

I recall one divorce client gave me a painting of two samurai warriors facing up to each other before engaging in battle. The client told me that it reminded her of me and my opponent standing outside the court waiting to go in. Another client gave me a drawing of two ladies sitting on either side of a table having coffee. Clearly one of them is describing her new boyfriend. The caption is "He's a lawyer - but for nice things." I like that. A number of clients were very generous and I recall once being given crates of oranges by a grateful client who worked at the old Covent Garden market; there were so many that just about everybody in the office went home with three or four. I also remember receiving two beautiful wine decanters and a very fine pocket watch from other grateful clients.

The most unusual gift that I ever received though was a bottle of whisky. I had represented a lady in her divorce and after the case was over I received a message that if I went to number ten Downing Street the following day I would find something there for my collection. I was convinced that this was a practical joke being played on me by one of my partners. I could not be sure though so off to Downing Street I went. When I arrived there I saw that there was a barrier across the end of the street and a policeman on duty. "I have something to collect from number 10 I said somewhat timidly. Instead of saying something like "Oh yeah" the policeman to my surprise just let me through. I approached number 10 and knocked on the famous door. It opened and the butler or whoever it was said "Can I help you sir?" Feeling rather foolish I said "Have you got something for collection by Mr Duncan?" "Just a moment sir" said the butler and he disappeared for a few moments and then returned with a package with my name on it. It was not a practical joke after all.

When I returned home that evening I opened the package and took out a bottle of House of Commons whisky that had been personally autographed by the then Prime Minister, Maggie Thatcher. Apparently my client's son - or it may have been a friend of his - worked at number 10 and had arranged the whole thing. What a great present. The whisky was very good and when I had finished the bottle I intended to keep it as a souvenir, but my wife who was no great supporter of Maggie Thatcher disposed of the empty bottle and I therefore lost my autograph as well.

I rather enjoyed acting in matrimonial disputes but I did find that many of my opponents were somewhat aggressive in their approach and tended to over identify with their clients. I regret to say that this was particularly true of lady solicitors acting for lady clients. One such I recall gave such a vivid and emotionally charged account of my client's alleged assault of his wife that supposedly took place in their bedroom that I asked her if she had been hiding in the cupboard! I on the other hand believed it was always better to keep one's cool and put forward one's client's case in a dispassionate way. I also believed that one should not antagonise the opposition without good reason. I like to think that by this attitude I helped to preserve better relations between divorcing parents which was of future benefit to them and particularly to their children, if they had any. I hope I am right in thinking I made a difference for the better.

CHAPTER FIVE

Other Areas of Law

Many years ago if I was asked on a social occasion what area of law I specialised in I would say litigation. This answer would make less sense today when so many solicitors specialise in quite narrow areas of the law. Within litigation today one could easily find solicitors specialising in medical negligence, employment rights, traffic accidents or defamation by way of example. Over my career I handled cases in virtually all branches of litigation. By way of example I dealt with accident claims, aircraft travel, bankruptcy, boundary disputes, commercial contracts, defamation, employment rights and intellectual property (primarily copyrights, patents and trademarks) as well as representing clients in the criminal and divorce courts. This made my professional life very varied indeed. I should however explain that I was able to do all of this by having a good general knowledge of the applicable law and then in appropriate cases by consulting a barrister who was a specialist in the particular subject matter.

I came across many odd or eccentric characters in my job. One of the earliest was a black African gentleman with the rather splendid name of Moses Fairchild Gohoho. Mr Gohoho had a dispute with one of my firm's clients. The case ended up in court and Mr Gohoho lost and was ordered to pay the costs. Payment was not made and to recover the money and to discourage Mr Gohoho from starting further court actions bankruptcy proceedings were instituted. There was an initial hearing before a bankruptcy judge and I attended to represent my client. When I arrived the court was already quite full. As the sitting was not due to start for some minutes I started doing "The Times" crossword. Mr Gohoho saw me hiding, he perhaps thought, behind my newspaper and said in a loud voice "Dat man, dat man over there is a crook" pointing at me.

I smiled and Mr Gohoho added "Dat's him, dat's him, the one with the smirk on his face." The other advocates found this somewhat funny and laughed at my discomfort. Just then the judge entered and as my case was first I had to address him with a somewhat red face. As far as I can recall this was the only time I was ever called a crook which is probably not the case for a friend of mine from university who actually practiced in a town called Crook. How often he must have been referred to as the crook solicitor!

Mr Gohoho achieved some notoriety in another case, not involving my firm, when he appeared in the Court of Appeal acting in person. Litigants who are not represented by lawyers sit in the very front of the court and on this particular day there were two, Mr Gohoho and a lady. Mr Gohoho had brought court proceedings which had resulted in a decision which was not to his liking. Mr Gohoho appealed and at the initial hearing of the appeal Mr Gohoho was ordered to pay £50 into court as security for the costs of the appeal - a decision with which he again did not agree. Mr Gohoho decided to protest and he accordingly took off his trousers and underpants and attired only in his shirt lay on the court bench. The female litigant, seeing what was happening, hastily retreated and the judge, who now realised what Mr Gohoho had done, ordered that the court be cleared whilst an official called the tipstaff removed Mr Gohoho from the court. For his contempt Mr Gohoho was sentenced to seven days imprisonment. For once the headline "a streaker in court" would not have referred to an incident at Wimbledon.

Another larger than life figure was Mr Gabriel Moschi who when I met him was also physically larger than most lives. Mr Moschi was managing director of a company called Rolloswin Investments Limited. On 20 October 1968 Mr Moschi met two directors of a Portuguese company called Chromolit Portugal. Mr Moschi's company was interested in buying

100,000 24 piece sets of cutlery and the Portuguese company were interested in selling such. A three page document was drawn up by Mr Moschi and signed by him and the two directors. When however the two directors returned to Portugal the other members of the board realised that the contract was not to their advantage and they disavowed it, claiming that it was not of legal effect as under their company rules more than two signatures were required to bind the company.

Unfortunately the judge found against my clients on this point. However we had a second argument which I believe to be of some interest. It came about in the following way. I was at a conference with the barrister I had instructed to represent the company when it suddenly occurred to me that the key meeting took place on a Sunday. I therefore suggested that we argue that the contract was unenforceable by reason of the Sunday Observance Act 1677. The Act stated that "all and every person and persons whatsoever shall on every Lord's day apply themselves to the observation of the same by exercising themselves thereon in the duties of piety and true religion.....and that no tradesman, artificer, workman, labourer or other person whatsoever, shall do or exercise any worldly labour, business or work of their ordinary callings, upon the Lord's day, or any part thereof..." The problem in applying this provision was that both parties were companies, so that we had to rely on the Interpretation Act 1889 which amongst other things declared that "the expression 'person' shall, unless the contrary intention appears, include a body corporate." There was a further difficulty in that in 1677 there were no limited companies similar to the modern version, although such bodies as the East India company, the Hudson's Bay company and a number of universities did exist.

In any event the judge decided that a limited company was incapable of public worship or attending church or exercising itself in the duties of piety and true religion on a Sunday or indeed on any other day of the week. Accordingly the decision went against my clients on this point too. I still think that as corporate bodies can only act through human beings (this was before computers were making decisions) the judge took too narrow a view of the law. Ironically the Sunday Observance Act 1677 was repealed on 1 January 1970 just over a month before the hearing of the Rolloswin case, so it was no longer the law when the case was decided. I have since often wondered if the fact that we had taken the point became known to the legislators, but perhaps the timing was just coincidental.

At the close of the hearing of the Rolloswin case the managing director of my client company insisted that we all went to dinner at a Japanese restaurant. It is not unusual to celebrate a win, but to be invited to dine after a loss was a new experience for me. The restaurant was situated just behind Selfridges and the food was very good, but I recall the evening because of two incidents that lightened the atmosphere. We were all seated on the floor and supplied with chopsticks. Clearly one of the directors of the Portugese company was unhappy with both arrangements. A waiter was called and at our request he brought some extra cushions and some cutlery. To everyone's amazement we found that the cutlery was manufactured by Chromolit Portugal itself. Later a trio of geisha girls entertained us by singing a traditional Japanese song. The first line of the first song which caused us to fall about laughing sounded just like "Moshe, moshe, moshe!"

Another interesting case involved clients of my firm who were Swiss bankers. I can give their name because the following events are all described in reported cases or happened in open court. Rahn & Bodmer, the Swiss bank, had dealings with English stockbrokers called T.C.Coombs. The bank paid T.C.Coombs 3 million Canadian dollars for some shares that turned out to be of no or little value. In the belief that T.C.Coombs were at fault the bank produced two fact setting documents, one of which they sent to the Serious Fraud Office (SFO) and the other to The Securities Association (TSA).

I became involved near the beginning and had a number of meetings at the SFO to discuss tactics. Their premises were in Elm Street and it was a well-worn joke that for suspected fraudsters going there for an interview was "A Nightmare on Elm Street" (the name of a current horror movie). After careful deliberation the SFO decided to prosecute the principals of T.C.Coombs. My job at that stage was to advise the bankers on the legal obligations of their directors and staff when appearing as witnesses in an English court and to attend court and take notes when they were giving evidence. This I duly did and the case moved on.

One day I received a telephone call from my contact at the SFO who said without any more explanation that I should make sure I attend court the next day. The case was being heard in the Middlesex Guildhall Crown Court, now the location of the Supreme Court. The court room was an impressive space and filled full. I sat quietly at the back expecting to have no part to play.

The barrister representing the defendants was making his closing address. Part of his argument was that the defendants had been set up. There was a conspiracy, said the defendants' barrister, to incriminate the defendants. He then stated who he contended were the parties to the conspiracy. They were, he said, the SFO itself, Mr Michael Birnbaum Q.C. (Counsel for the SFO) and the bank's solicitor, Mr Stuart Duncan. To say that I was astonished would be a complete understatement. In the end the defendants were not in fact convicted, but the reason for their acquittal was due to the unsatisfactory quality of the evidence against them rather than, I am happy to say, because of their conspiracy allegations.

Accident claims could on occasion be interesting to handle, but I always found it hard dealing with people whose lives had been so sadly altered, often through no fault of their own. I remember a client who had lost her sense of taste and smell after being knocked off her bike. After a conference with the barrister I had instructed we went to a pub near the barrister's chambers to discuss the implications of the advice received and I asked my client what she wanted to drink "It doesn't matter" she said "It all tastes the same." I am glad though to say that she won her case and we recovered satisfactory damages.

Another case involved an unfortunate young man who could only remember most things for about 15 minutes. I remember being told that he had lots of videos which he could keep on watching because he never could recall what happened next. Again I am glad to say that we won the case and recovered substantial damages. In this particular case the damages were paid by way of a structured settlement which was a new thing in those days. By arrangement with the defendants an insurance company put forward a plan for monthly payments for life with uplifts because of inflation and occasional capital injections for specific likely requirements. This avoided the danger of a lump sum being squandered or it running out over a long lifetime. I believe of the first hundred structured settlements that were agreed I was the only solicitor who had ushered more than one through the courts. The other structured settlement I handled involved a lady who became a paraplegic - another tragic case.

One slightly unusual case I handled involved a minor traffic accident. The driver whose car was damaged was driving along the motorway behind a sort of camper van. The van had a bed on a higher level, but the top of the van in which the bed was located was not securely attached to the base of the van. Accordingly when the driver slammed on his brakes the top of the top of the van came adrift and the driver behind suddenly saw a bed coming towards him some four feet off the ground. The bed made contact but fortunately, as far as I can remember, there were no serious injuries.

Neighbour disputes could be quite vicious and I often advised that consideration should be given to moving house. This advice though was not well received. "Why should I" was the typical response. I recall one case where in the dead of night one house owner would lean out of her window with long cutters and snip the heads off her neighbour's prize sunflowers. In a similar case another house owner also at night sprayed her neighbour's flower border with weed killer destroying all her plants. These acts of senseless damage were usually accompanied by verbal abuse during daylight hours. Unfortunately a tit for tat situation could easily arise when things would go from bad to worse. Court proceedings rarely solved the problem and unless one or the other moved the misery usually continued.

Because tempers often ran high it was not unusual for clients involved in neighbour disputes (and this applied to other areas of law as well) to ask me to take some action as a matter of principle. My usual response was to ask the client if he or she was prepared to pay let us say £500 on account of the costs to be incurred. "That's fine" was the usual reply. I would then say "And are you prepared to pay £1000 on account?" There was normally a pause and the client would then usually say "O.K." "Good" I would say "And are you prepared to pay £2000 on account?" "What's going on?" the client would now respond. "I just wish to know" I would say "when principles come to a stop and economics take over."

I did not do much licensing work but I was peripherally involved in one case at the beginning of my career. One of my partners was acting for somebody who wanted an off licence and the application was to be dealt with at Billericay magistrates court. I had posted some document and simply had to give evidence of that fact. I was the only witness, as far as I can recall, and I duly went into what if the court had been sitting as a criminal court would have been the dock. I gave my name and occupation and explained how I had posted the particular document. My evidence over I returned to my place. The court then asked if anybody objected to the granting of the off licence and a woman stood up. The magistrate said "You can either give your objection from where you are or you can go over there", pointing to the dock I had just occupied. "Oh I am not going over there" she said "that's for criminals." I know the public has always had a poor impression of solicitors, but this was going a bit far.

On a number of occasions I appeared in the coroner's court, usually on behalf of the relatives of the deceased person. My instructions often were to try and prevent a finding of suicide in cases where this was a possible conclusion. Generally the family did not like the stigma and there were cases where such a finding would void an insurance policy on the deceased. Sometimes a note left by the deceased was ambiguous. I recall one case where the deceased left a note which read "I am leaving for good" and then drove his car off a bridge. Had the deceased committed suicide or was he hurrying away from his wife to start a new life when he lost control of his car was the question. I think I am right in recalling that we avoided a finding of suicide in that case.

An unusual case was a poor man who was sprinkling bone meal on his garden on a windy day. The man inadvertently inhaled some of the fine powder and within an hour or so he was dead. The bone meal imported from Africa and sold through garden shops in England contained bones from cows that suffered from anthrax. I did some research and discovered that on average there is one death from anthrax in England every five years. My client's husband was very unlucky. My main role in this case was to pressurise the wholesalers and retailers into withdrawing their stocks and informing the public of the risks that using this product entailed. I was able to do this and as far as I know there were no other casualties.

Property disputes did not generally throw up many interesting memories, but I do recall a secretarial error in one case that amused me at the time. The building in question had some sort of rot and I dictated a report in which I stated that "There was algae behind the wallpaper." This when typed read "Algy behind the wallpaper." I told my secretary that she had misspelled "algae", but she said that this was in fact just her misunderstanding. My secretary explained that she thought that "Algy" was a dog that had somehow torn the wallpaper and got behind it!

Near the beginning of my career I did have an interesting property dispute. I acted for a lady who had a farm in Surrey. Next to the farm was a piece of land that her neighbour had sold off to a developer. The developer then built a number of houses whose gardens backed on to my client's land. The houses were sold to various different purchasers who no doubt were looking forward to a peaceful life in the country. One day shortly after his purchase one of the house owners looked out of his window and saw a lady in his garden trimming his hedge. Somewhat astonished the owner went to remonstrate, but the lady farmer explained that it was her hedge as was the land on which she was standing. The owner backed off for the moment and went to check on his Land Certificate. This showed that he owned the property right up to the hedge. Reassured the owner took on the lady farmer again, but she insisted that she owned the disputed land and that her once neighbour must have sold land to the developer that he himself did not in fact own. The Latin maxim for this is nemo dat quod non habet which can be translated in the words of the song as "I can't give you what I haven't got."

The dispute went to court and our case depended in part on what is called the hedge and ditch presumption. The theory of this is that where on the boundary of land there is a hedge and a ditch there is a presumption that the boundary is the edge of the ditch that is furthest from the hedge. The reason behind this is that it is presumed that the land owner went to the furthest extent of his land to dig the ditch and then threw back the dug soil on to his own land rather than on to his neighbour's land thus creating a bank on which he then plants his hedge. Our difficulty was that the ditch, if there had ever been one, was no longer. However I found a local man who remembered the ditch and it being filled in. Our next problem was that he was over 90 and in poor health. Although we took a sworn statement from him it was important to get to trial before he met his maker. I believe my memory is right in recalling that we just made it. In any event we won our case and the new neighbours had to seek recompense from the developer who sold them their houses. I must say though that I did have some sympathy with the owners of the new houses who in my view were not entirely unreasonable in not wanting their farming neighbour going into their gardens at will.

A property dispute that was also interesting legally concerned a country house that a client of my firm bought in the Home Counties. The selling agents had described the house as "a fine Lutyens property". About nine months after the purchase our client had to see his doctor or it might have been his dentist and whilst he was in the waiting room he was looking through "Country Life." In the magazine our client was surprised to find an article about country houses in England that were alleged to have been designed by Edwin

Lutyens, the famous architect, but in fact were not. One house the author said that was almost certainly wrongly attributed to Lutyens was - and he then gave the name of our client's house.

The client as a result took proceedings against the selling agents and I believe, if I recall correctly, the sellers as well. The main problem was, if the house was not a Lutyens house, whether our client had suffered any financial loss. If our client had paid what any other purchaser might have paid for the house the answer was arguably no. If however our client had paid a premium because of the Lutyens name then that sum could arguably determine our client's loss. I recall a half day spent at the Royal Institute of British Architects' library researching into who the real architect might be. I concluded that it was likely to be a Philip Tilden, but I could not prove this. Although the case proceeded to a court hearing the interesting legal point was never resolved as after a couple of days the parties came to a private agreement.

Another case that had an interesting legal point that was never resolved concerned a cargo vessel that was in the Mediterranean on a beautiful clear day. Another large vessel approached and I was later told that when they were a quarter of a mile apart the crew went on deck to watch the collision - it was too late to be avoided. Both vessels were badly damaged and the other vessel decided to put in to the harbour at Alexandria. Unfortunately the harbour master refused to let the vessel in to harbour because the size of the ship meant that it would likely damage the harbour bottom. The ship therefore set out to sea again and a storm came up and it sank. The point of interest was whether our clients were responsible for the shipwreck or had the consequences of their negligence been severed by the negligence of the other ship's captain in making for the wrong harbour. At the trial however the other vessel was held to have been responsible for the initial collision, so the point did not come up for decision.

Reverting to property law I recall that a landlord and tenant dispute near the beginning of my career did cause me some problems. I was acting for the landlord and had gone to a county court to obtain possession of a particular property from a tenant who had not paid his rent. In county courts solicitors can be identified by their wearing a black gown and a wing collar with two white tabs. I was waiting for my case to come on when a young woman carrying a baby approached me. She was in considerable distress. "I have a baby" she said "and my landlord is trying to evict me. I can't afford a lawyer. Please help me." "I am sorry" I said "but I am waiting for my case to come on." "Please" she said. "All right" I replied "I shall just look at your papers." I did this and to my surprise I discovered that the client I was there to represent was her landlord too. For some reason though he had not instructed me in this other case. I could not in the circumstances formally represent the mother, but I did put her plight to my client in a sympathetic way and he gave her more time to pay her rent arrears. So all was well that ended well, but in future I decided that I would probably not help when approached by a stranger outside a courtroom.

In recalling being involved with both sides, I am reminded of a story I was told of a barrister who took things much too casually. I believe it may have been the same gentleman who featured in my recollection of the client who was sentenced to four years in prison. The barrister was instructed to appear for the prosecution in a magistrates court on a number of small fairly simple cases. Indeed he thought they were so simple that he had only glanced at his briefs. There were about a dozen briefs, all involving the same type of offence. When about the fourth case was called on the barrister stood up and said as he had before "And I appear for the prosecution, your worships" and sat down. The defendant was then called but nobody responded. Whilst waiting the barrister used the time to look at the other briefs and to his horror found that the name of the defendant who had just been called was on one of them. The barrister's clerk had in error accepted instructions from both sides. The barrister had to stand up again. Considerably embarrassed he said "And I also appear for the defendant your worships." I am sorry to say that my laughter interrupted the story teller and I never found out what happened next.

One interesting and unusual case that came my way concerned Verdi's opera Aida. As a keen operagoer it had extra interest for me. In the late eighties a Swedish company produced a film of the opera based on a stage production by the Stockholm Folk Opera. The opera was sung in Swedish and filmed in Lanzarote. The male lead Radames was played by a dancer with somebody else singing his part and the slave girls were all topless. It was completely different from anything that I had ever seen at Covent Garden. The issue in the case concerned insurance of the box office receipts and I had to view a video version to see how the film compared with the description of it given by my clients to the insurance company. I took the video home and was watching the film when my wife came in. I had just reached the point where the topless slave girls were performing a somewhat erotic dance on sun baked sand. "What are you doing?" my wife said. "Please do not disturb me" I replied "I am busy working." I do wonder now whether this explanation was in fact accepted.

Certainly the Aida video was more interesting than another one I took home from the office to watch. The camera was underwater and was pointed at the legs of an oil rig. Attempts were being made to carry out repairs underwater by a robot. The definition was not good and there was very little to see through the murky water. It required considerable willpower to watch this video which if I remember correctly ran for over two hours. In any event this time my wife left me undisturbed.

An interesting and at the time important case was Thrustcode v WW Computing Limited. Thrustcode had invented a system for managing production of articles, let us say wooden furniture. Here the key elements would be what orders do you have and anticipate having, how much wood do you keep in stock, what sort of machines will be needed and when and what staff will be required.

Thrustcode realised that the system was more readily saleable as a computer program and the company engaged a contractor to write such a program. The contractor did as asked and then his company WW Computing produced a rival product using the same system. This was in the early days of computers and the relevant law was by no means clear. I acted for Thrustcode and we applied for an injunction to stop WW Computing marketing their product.

The case came before Vice Chancellor Megarry, a highly respected judge. Megarry V C started the hearing somewhat ominously by saying that he knew very little about computers. We produced evidence to show that if you ran both programs on a computer and printed off the pages of the two programs they were virtually identical. Clearly the contractor had copied Thrustcode's product. We succeeded in that Megarry V C held that a computer program was capable of protection as a literary work, but we failed in getting an injunction. The reason for our failure is that WW Computing had used a different source code to Thrustcode. The "language" of the two programs was different even though once on computer they were converted into virtually identical texts. Megarry V C said in his judgment that one must not confuse the results that come about by operating the program with the program itself as to which copyright is claimed. Megarry V C gave an arithmetical example; he pointed out that one could arrive at the number 4 by adding 2 and 2, by multiplying 2 by 2 and by calculating what 2 per cent of 200 comes to. Megarry V C concluded that a number of different processes could produce the same answer but still remain different processes that have not involved any copying. I thought at the time that this was a restrictive approach; legislation has now given greater protection - but too late alas for my client.

One gentleman whose case I did not take on felt for reasons I cannot now recall that he had been insulted by the Prime Minister who was then Harold Macmillan. The gentleman wanted to sue the British government for one million pounds - a lot of money in those days. The case was without any foundation and I suggested as delicately as possible that perhaps the gentleman needed a doctor more than a solicitor. This suggestion did not go down well and the potential client produced a small knife and thrust it into my desk to make his point, saying that it was a solicitor not a doctor that he wanted. I declined to act saying that I was too busy to do his case justice. Fortunately the gentleman left quietly, although my secretary was somewhat alarmed at the noise and even more so when she saw the knife marks on my desk. Oddly I never felt in any danger despite the fact that there are many examples of lawyers being attacked by irate opponents or indeed on occasion by irate clients.

Bringing law suits seems to appeal to those with disturbed minds and I was involved with a number of litigants over the years, acting for or more usually against such persons. In retrospect the mental state of the individual is often clear, but at the outset often much less so. One very plausible lady brought over a dozen actions against doctors and solicitors (including my firm). When I first met her, which was after she had sued us, I tried to settle the dispute but I was wasting my time. Clearly this lady enjoyed bringing court actions and nothing I might have said or done was going to stop her. Such persons can be declared by the court to be vexatious litigants whereafter they need the permission of the court to bring any action. This restriction would have been fine were it not for the fact that the court generally required the litigant to have started a large number of spurious actions before making such an order. I am now not sure what happened in the case in question but I believe the claim was later struck out.

One of my clients, an airline, also suffered from customers with somewhat deranged views. One customer I recall brought proceedings against my clients because when the plane he was travelling on approached Rio de Janeiro it started to bank steeply. The customer was frightened by this manoeuvre and complained that it affected the whole of his stay in Brazil and prevented him from finalising a book which would have made him a great deal of money. As I know from personal experience if the plane does not bank steeply when approaching Rio airport, it would crash into the mountains. It was a ridiculous claim and after some difficulties I had it struck out.

Many claims on airlines relate to delays in departure, but oddly one of the cases I dealt with for the same airline related to two lady passengers who complained that their plane left too early. What happened was that all the passengers had checked in when the pilot realised that a storm was approaching and that it was unlikely that the plane would be able to take off at the scheduled time. The pilot decided that the best option was to leave early and get ahead of the storm. Accordingly a tannoy message went out, but the two lady passengers in question were enjoying themselves in the airport bar and did not hear it. The plane left without them. Now in some airports this would have been a minor inconvenience, but at this rather small airport there were at the time few flights per week and as far as I can recall the two ladies were stranded for two or three days. Their claim I should add was unsuccessful.

Although I later qualified as an arbitrator, I did not often appear as an advocate at arbitration hearings. One I do though recall was held in a hotel in Gloucester. I believe I acted for an architect who was in dispute with his client, a lady who owned a chemists shop. The hearing lasted three days and on the last day to try and finish the case that day we all agreed to carry on without stopping for lunch. The hotel provided us with sandwiches and tea and the pharmacist, being the only woman present, volunteered to pour the tea out. I was at the time addressing the arbitrator and I recall I was submitting that the lady pharmacist had told a number of lies when giving her evidence. I was briefly interrupted by the lady herself who sweetly asked "one lump or two?" I did wonder if she was referring to arsenic rather than sugar, but I survived so it must have just been sugar. This I do remember, but who won the case I do not now recall.

One case where my efforts had a wide impact concerned the attempts of the Central Electricity Generating Board to put up electricity pylons close to Box Hill, a beauty spot in Surrey. A number of local residents formed a group that opposed what they considered would be a blight on the countryside. The views from Box Hill and other high points would be adversely affected by the sight of these large structures. The Board were not prepared to agree to put the cables underground because the cost was, if I remember correctly, ten times as much. Accordingly the issue went to a public enquiry and I was instructed to represent the Pylon Action Group. I carried out, with the assistance of the local residents, a good deal of research and I then instructed a prominent Queen's Counsel to attend the enquiry which took place in Dorking in Surrey. I am glad to say that our efforts were completely successful and the cables had to go underground despite the extra cost. Oddly it has taken me over 25 years since the enquiry to revisit the area and stand at the top of Box Hill and take in the splendid view. As I stood there I was quietly satisfied with my contribution to preserving an uncluttered view for all to enjoy.

At an earlier stage in my career I remember appearing at a public enquiry into whether plans to build a sports building in a North London park should go ahead or not. I was instructed by a local resident to oppose the proposal and I duly turned up at Finchley town hall. I remember little of the enquiry now save for my asking questions of the local lord mayor who said that as a youngster he used to cycle down a particular path into the playing fields. I said that I thought cycling on this path was prohibited and the mayor had to admit that he had broken the law. The inspector found in favour of the proposal, but through lack of funds the project was never implemented. Ironically when I later came to live in East Finchley my children often played in the playground where the sports building would have stood.

I have recounted in various places in this book cases that had an international element. In looking back three more of such cases come to mind.

One of my earliest international cases involved a contract between a British company and the military of a country in South America (I have forgotten which). The South Americans committed a breach of contract and I was asked to advise the British company. I must have been rather naive at the time because I was quite shocked at the bribery that the British company had to engage in to procure the contract in the first place.

I was told by my clients that first it was necessary to bribe a sergeant with let us say a crate of wine. For that the sergeant would introduce the company to a captain. The captain would then be given let us say a motorbike. For that the captain would introduce the company to a general. One morning the general would wake up and looking out of his window see let us say a brand new motor car. The general would drive off with a large smile on his face and then he would later advise his colleagues that the British company were the best applicants for the job. I can remember being told this now, but I am less clear on how matters concluded. I rather think that my clients were unsuccessful in their negotiations and decided against going to court. Bringing court actions in South America at that time was lengthy, costly and the result problematic to say the least.

Not long after the end of communism in the Soviet Union one of my partners had a British businessman as a client who was trying to strike a deal with a group of Russians concerning some airplanes stationed in an airfield somewhere abroad. The partner who was holding a meeting in our offices asked me to join him and I recall going into a smoke filled room. The Russians were a tough looking lot and I was - rightly as it later turned out - suspicious of the whole thing. The Russians' lawyer was a very unusual solicitor who after the meeting told me that he had to hurry away because he was a white witch and had a meeting of witches to attend. If anybody else but he had said this I would have taken it as a joke, but he was absolutely serious. However the main reason I recall the meeting is that during it this solicitor kept on giving some advice that one of the Russians clearly did not like. Eventually the Russian could take no more and he turned around and punched the solicitor quite hard on the jaw. Amazingly the solicitor took this in his stride and the meeting continued. I was at the time very glad that this blow did not lead to a general fistfight because the Russians looked highly capable of inflicting serious damage.

My firm's strong link with Portugal also provided me with a number of cases over many years. These involved for instance contracts between British and Portuguese businessmen (such as the Chromolit Portugal case referred to above). Many of these breach of contract cases related to the sale and purchase of textiles and at one time I knew something about warps and wefts, but it is all now forgotten. Some cases were about road accidents or other mishaps that affected British people living in or holidaying in Portugal. I recall for example advising on road accidents in Estoril and Funchal. By chance I later happened to visit both locations. I travelled to Lisbon on business on a number of occasions and I once travelled to Porto - another fine city - to give advice on some contractual dispute.

One Portuguese client though I remember particularly well. The client was actually due to see one of my partners, but I just happened to notice her sitting in the waiting room. I recall an attractive lady who was wearing a rather flimsy pink dress with a large hat; she also had on a strong perfume. My younger partner saw the client in his office, but after about ten minutes he left the client on her own and came into my office to seek my advice. The problem, he said, is that the client wanted to update her passport, but the Portuguese State had told her that she must wait until the passport expires. "Why can't she just wait" I responded unhelpfully. My partner said "Well, just look at her passport photograph." I did and there was a photograph of a slightly rough looking seaman complete with tattoo. The client had apparently undergone a sex change operation and was finding travelling between countries with such a passport an embarrassing experience. We made some enquiries of the Portuguese authorities, but they were intransigent and our poor client just had to wait until the renewal date some years ahead. Whether the State then accepted the client's new status I never discovered.

As a result of the Portuguese connection I became a committee member of the Portuguese chamber of commerce in London. I remember the meetings with some fondness, because as well as the friendliness of the other committee members the meetings were enhanced by our ending them by drinking some excellent Portuguese wines that one of the committee, a wine merchant, brought along. At various times I gave legal advice to the chamber and oddly I was later asked to give legal advice to the Spanish chamber of commerce in London as well - an Iberian double of which I am proud. Looking back I consider myself very lucky to have been a solicitor at a time when having such a wide base of work was still possible. How much more interesting I think it was, for me anyway, to advise a divorce client in the morning and then to represent another client on a criminal charge in the magistrates court in the afternoon; or to attend a conference with counsel on a case of copyright infringement during another morning and then to advise a client who had suffered injuries in a factory accident during another afternoon. One had to be quick witted and often quick footed, but that was part of the challenge and part of the fun.

Looking back it seems now as if it all should have been rather stressful, but I believe that most of the time I found the stress a stimulant rather than a depressant. The only real legacy I have been left with, as I have mentioned in a different context, is an antipathy to answering the telephone or indeed to making telephone calls if I can get away with it. Overall I enjoyed my career as a solicitor and my second career as an employment judge about which I shall write later in this book.

CHAPTER SIX

PALS

After the merger with Stoneham & Sons I started to do more international work. This involved cases where there was an international element (such as disputes arising out of contracts made in England that had to be performed in another country, British subjects having accidents abroad or divorces between couples born or brought up in different countries), but it also included appointing local lawyers abroad to act as our agents and referring clients to the most suitable lawyers in other countries where we could not handle their cases from England. We took over from Stoneham & Sons a large book full of the names and addresses of recommended foreign lawyers, but it soon became apparent to me that there were a number of significant countries where we had no established contacts at all.

Soon after the merger I was asked by a client about the law of Zanzibar on a particular topic. I did not dare to admit that, as well as not knowing what legal system Zanzibar operated under, I did not really know where it was. In such cases Martindale-Hubbell was invaluable. This American publication not only listed law firms worldwide, but it also provided a brief statement of the basic law on a variety of subjects for each country. Clearly this was generally insufficient to give definitive advice, but it regularly gave one a starting point and some indication of the type of legal system in operation.

The absence of established contacts did not matter so much out of Europe, but I did feel that we should have reliable contacts in the major European countries. I therefore made a list of the important countries in Europe where the firm had no or no established contacts and I suggested to my partners that we should remedy the situation. This proposal, I was pleased to discover, met with general approval and it was decided that a team consisting of three partners should travel around Europe visiting as well as our existing legal contacts other law firms to whom we could hopefully refer work with confidence. John Nilsson was the lead partner and I was deputed to travel with him around Northern and North Eastern Europe. This would take a week and then another partner, Nicholas Lane, was to join John Nilsson in visiting law firms in the rest of Europe. This would take a further week.

As the original idea of establishing a network of reliable contacts was mine I was given the planning to do. To start with Stonehams' former partners in their Lisbon office were contacted to see who they referred work to elsewhere in Europe. I then checked with the firm's bankers to see who they sent their European legal work to and I researched in Martindale-Hubbell for European law firms that did international work and were somewhat comparable in size. Finally I ended up with a list of cities and with two or three law firms in each city to visit. This list included places where we already had established contacts as I considered it prudent to look for alternatives in case of need. Eventually I had a draft itinerary which my partners approved. My hard working secretary then had the task of fixing all the appointments and making sure we had time to get from place to place. Our usual travel agent then sorted out the flights and we were ready to go. Although I had travelled abroad on many previous occasions this was something quite different and I was greatly looking forward to it.

I believe it was in March 1974 that John Nilsson and I flew to Oslo. The plane went via Stavanger for some reason that I do not now recall. I do however remember that it was a Sunday and that the weather was pretty crisp. Oslo is, compared with other capital cities, fairly small and it is a city I enjoy visiting, particularly because the Norwegians are very friendly and very pro English - at least they were then and I hope that our football hooligans have not since spoiled that good relationship.

If I recall correctly we visited three law firms in Oslo and all I can now really remember is that after the third interview we went for a drink with the senior partner in that particular firm who asked us where we were off to next. We told him that we had appointments in Stockholm and he said that he would be very interested in who we selected as our representative there. This query, simple though it was, later gave birth to "the grand plan."

We then journeyed on to Stockholm, a beautiful city often described as "the Venice of the North." Malmo, also in Sweden, was next and after a brief stay there we were off on the ferry to Copenhagen, another very attractive city. In each city we visited a number of law firms. It was all pretty hectic and my recollections now are somewhat sparse, but I do recall having an excellent evening meal (probably some kind of herring which they prepare wonderfully well) in an open air section of a pretty restaurant in the Tivoli Gardens in Copenhagen.

Our next port of call was Hamburg where, as was usual, we called on three law firms. There had been little time on this trip so far to look at the sights. However John and I did decide to see Hamburg by night. The centre of the town appeared to be within walking distance from the hotel and so off we started. After a short time we realised that we were going in the wrong direction and I therefore stopped a man and in my very limited German I asked him the way to the centre of the city. Clearly my German was deficient because the man thought that we were looking for a sex club and insisted on giving my partner a card to a club called "The Venus Bar."

John put this in his breast pocket and forgot all about it, which was unfortunate for him because when that suit came to be cleaned his wife found it and he had some explaining to do! In any event we found our way to the Reeperbahn, Hamburg's famous street of somewhat dubious entertainment, and had a drink or two in the Hofbrauhaus. This was a beer house with a typical German oompah band. One difference though was that visitors were invited up to conduct the band which then played a piece that had some relevance to their own country. John was at some point called up and he conducted "Roll out the Barrel" with great gusto.

The next city we visited was Frankfurt and after our appointments John and I had dinner in an open air restaurant in the Old Town. John thought that he was playing safe by having cold meats whereas I had spicy local sausages and sauerkraut. Needless to say the next day I felt fine whereas John was distinctly queasy. This was unfortunate as we were due to fly to Luxembourg that morning for the last series of visits that I would be involved with.

John and I arrived at Frankfurt airport an hour and a quarter early. We were only carrying hand luggage (cleverly designed cases that took a suit without creasing it and small enough to be carried on board) to avoid having to wait for our luggage on arrival. In those days, before more careful security precautions came in, we should have had more than sufficient time. However John was moving somewhat gingerly and when we reached the check in desk there was a long queue so that we did not reach the plane door until 10 minutes before take-off. We moved forward - only 15 feet to go - when a rather formidable and sour looking German air stewardess said "You are late and cannot board." I said that we only had hand baggage and it would only take a moment to get on, but she was implacable and waved us away.

98

Unfortunately there were no other flights to Luxembourg that day, so I abandoned John and rather than returning to the hotel took a plane home to Heathrow instead. I did though decide to put a curse on the officious air stewardess to become effective if I never got to Luxembourg before my sixtieth birthday: in fact she was spared because I did get there some years later. John stayed over in Frankfurt and went on to Luxembourg the following day and then, if I remember correctly, he and Nicholas Lane, who joined up with him, went on to Amsterdam, Brussels, Paris, Zurich, Rome and Madrid.

Most of the lawyers we called on greeted us with great warmth and great interest. Many of them impressed us, but especially impressive was their almost universal command of the English language. At the end of each day John and I independently dictated on tape our initial thoughts about the law firms we had visited that day. With one exception we were unanimous as to which law firm to recommend to our partners and after further discussion between us we were able to resolve which of the two firms we disagreed about should be in our final choice.

The European trip was a very interesting experience and it lived up to all of my expectations. All of the cities I visited were new to me and thus it was something of an adventure as well. It was though pretty intense, involving lots of flights, lots of hotels and meeting lots of new people. I do not now remember feeling so but I suspect that I must have been fairly tired when I returned to my office on the following Monday morning.

When we were all back in England the team of the three of us prepared a report to the other partners giving our recommendations as to which law firms we should approach for further cooperation. Then the query by the Oslo lawyer set

John Nilsson and I thinking that perhaps we could set up a law club of European lawyers who had an international outlook. This today is pretty commonplace, but in 1974 it was a fairly novel idea. Indeed I believe we were one of the first English law firms to found such a club. Fortunately our partners were in agreement with our proposals and John and I were given the go ahead. First though we had to contact all the law firms and get their reactions. We duly did this and the response from each law firm was very positive. We therefore arranged for a meeting of all of the law firms to take place in London when we could decide if and if so how to move forward.

The London meeting took place in October 1974 and there was unanimous approval that a law club should be formed consisting initially of those law firms present and also law firms in Rome and Zurich whose principals had not been able to attend the meeting. The next question was what to call ourselves. There were some moments of contemplation and then one of the Dutch lawyers, who had been educated in England, said "Why not call ourselves PALS which denotes the best of friends and could stand for Private Association of Lawyers." Somebody pointed out that it was also the name of a dog food and I believe somebody else said that in his country it was the name of a contraceptive. Despite these to me valid objections the acronym was unanimously approved and PALS we all became.

It was agreed that meetings should take place every six months and that the members should try and refer legal work to each other if possible. One of the Danish lawyers (we thought of him as "The Viking", primarily because of his splendid ginger beard) then said that he would be happy to welcome us to Copenhagen for the next meeting. PALS was on its way. The idea had become a reality and rather like a snowball it got bigger and bigger as it was rolled forward!

Future meetings were attended generally by one, two or sometimes three lawyers from each law firm who were, with one exception, all male. The Brussels law firm was initially headed by a man, but the second partner was a lady and she came on her own after her senior colleague had passed away. Spouses usually accompanied the lawyers and these were therefore all wives except for the one solitary husband. A pattern in due course emerged of meeting up on a Thursday evening for a meal and then for the lawyers Friday was a working day followed by a formal meal in the evening. On Saturday the host law firm took the group somewhere interesting for the day and this was followed by an impromptu meal in the evening. Some members flew home on the Saturday evening, but many stayed on for further sightseeing and returned home on the Sunday afternoon. The spouses were entertained on the Friday by the host law firm and visited palaces, castles, art galleries and suchlike. The working day consisted of general discussion about matters of mutual interest and there were papers on particular legal subjects that would be of interest to international lawyers. It soon became clear that we all faced similar problems in practising law, but the solutions that we reached were often quite different. This was often because of the different attitudes displayed in each country by the profession's governing body or because of the position in which lawyers were held by the public.

Copenhagen was a successful meeting, but at the working session it soon became apparent that there would be restrictions on our mutual cooperation. The vast majority of the members said that their names could not be mentioned on another member's notepaper or in a law directory entry - only the city or town could be stated as a place where a contact existed. The cities where the law firms practised that were represented at this meeting were London, Amsterdam,

Brussels Copenhagen, Frankfurt, Hamburg, Lisbon, Luxembourg, Madrid, Malmo, Oslo, Paris and Stockholm.

When in Copenhagen I took the opportunity to see the Little Mermaid, the statue based on Hans Christian Andersen's story, which really is little being around about five feet high and looking much smaller from a distance. I also remember climbing the golden staircase that winds around the spire of Our Saviour's Church. At the top, after climbing 400 steps, 150 of which were outside, both I and my colleague John Nilsson were affected by vertigo whereas to our chagrin neither wife was affected at all. We also went with our Viking host and his wife to The Royal Deer Park where there was, as well as deer, possibly the oldest funfair in the world. It was established on a small scale as far back as 1583 and just grew and grew. On reaching the rollercoaster our hosts said that they regularly had a ride and not wishing to let the side down we agreed to join them. The Danish lawyer slipped away to buy the tickets and as we climbed aboard I realised that he and his wife were remaining on solid ground. I said "Aren't you coming?" and our Viking host said "Oh no, we've been on it many times." We had been had! The contraption was built of wood and had many tunnels which were completely dark; accordingly when going through a tunnel you did not know if you would come out pushing upwards or plunging downwards. The whole thing shook and was quite terrifying. Frankly our party were very glad to get back on to terra firma.

I missed the next meeting which was in Paris at the end of October 1975. This coincided with the merger of Stonehams & Pumfreys with J.D.Langton & Passmore, a law firm practising in Bolton Street, Mayfair, and our move to that address. It was a very busy period. Our Orpington office had by that time gone, but the merger brought us offices in Saffron Walden in Essex and Ashford in Kent and about a year later a firm practising in Chislehurst in Kent also joined us. With the

102

Croydon office going strong we now had a number of branch offices (a mixed blessing).

The move from Great Marlborough Street to Bolton Street relieved us from having to occupy glass boxes that were too cold in the winter, too hot in the summer and too small all year round. J.D.Langton & Passmore were a well-established firm and our two practices fitted together very well. J.D Langton & Passmore used to act for a large number of well-known actors and actresses and still had many clients in the entertainment business.

I was, though, particularly envious of the fact that the firm had acted for Princess Youssoupoff in her famous case against M.G.M. In the film "Rasputin, the Mad Monk" a female character was shown to have had sexual relations with Rasputin. Princess Youssoupoff claimed that she was identifiable as the character depicted and that it was defamatory to represent her as having been seduced. M.G.M. in their defence argued that the film actually showed the female character being raped and that as that did not show any fault on her part it could not be defamatory. The judge disagreed and contended that whether it was seduction or ravishment it was defamatory and he awarded substantial damages. The case is well known to law students today as the judge also decided that defamation in a film was libel ("written") rather than slander ("spoken") - the first time this point had been decided. What a great case to be instructed to handle, involving interesting legal points as well as a fascinating period of Russian history.

Mayfair would now be my professional home for the next 20 years and I am glad to say that my new office was a great improvement on its predecessor. The building in Bolton Street was somewhat old-fashioned, but it had some charm and not being almost next door to the London Palladium gave it a more professional feel. Bolton Street itself was a fairly undistinguished street but as a monopoly player as a child I felt that I had moved round the board to the most exclusive site, Mayfair.

Close to our offices was Shepherd Market where Ye Grapes public house was the favoured office watering place. Shepherd Market also had some fine restaurants and wine bars. It was in those days notorious for the ladies who walked the streets seeking business and it was not unusual to be accosted. One of my partners who was somewhat diffident told me that he was walking in Shepherd Market late one morning when a young woman in knee high black boots had asked him if he wanted a good time. "What did you say?" I asked him. "I told her that I hadn't even had my lunch yet" he replied. I had no answer to that.

Most of the attendants at the PALS meetings were commercial lawyers so as a litigator I had less in common with them than my commercial partners. For this reason and because it was important for my new partners to meet the partners in the European law firms I missed a number of PALS meetings. Indeed the next meeting I attended was in London in October 1977. I did though some work in the background such as drafting a PALS directory. The various law firms' initial reluctance to their firm names appearing in any kind of directory had by this time somewhat evaporated. Three years on things had changed and the idea of lawyers advertising their services was no longer unacceptable.

At the London meeting representatives from the law firms in the cities I have already mentioned were present as well as representatives from law firms in Athens, Vienna and Zurich. This was my first sight of our Greek associate. He was a larger than life character with flamboyant gestures and a resounding voice - in my view he would have been a better casting for Zorba the Greek than Anthony Quinn. Our Athenian friend was a bachelor of advanced years who impressed all the male lawyers by producing a small notebook in any city we visited and, after checking, saying that there was a lady living there that he just must call on; he would then disappear for some hours.

PALS had a number of characters amongst the various lawyers who attended our meetings. I have already mentioned our Greek colleague and our Viking colleague with the ginger beard from Copenhagen. Then there was the Dutch lawyer who could beat any of the English lawyers on quotations from Shakespeare. Whilst recalling foreigners' knowledge of English literature I should also mention the Finnish lawyer from a firm who joined us later. He said to me at one meeting that he been sitting up in bed the previous night reading an English book of essays from a publication called "The Spectator", but he had forgotten the name of the 18th century author. I suggested Richard Steele and he agreed that was who it was. I did not tell him that I had only ever read Steele's essays for my O levels (the predecessor of the GCSE and taken at about 16 years of age). One of the German lawyers once asked me who my favourite German author was. I think I said Thomas Mann and then prayed that he would not ask me which of his works I preferred. This would have been difficult to answer as I had not read any.

It is truly humbling meeting intelligent people from mainland Europe who speak excellent English and have a real understanding of English writers whereas I (and I suspect many other Englishmen) do not have a second language and have a fairly limited knowledge of European literature. In fact I found virtually all of my European colleagues stimulating company. There was an extremely good fellowship throughout my association with the club, despite the past history of difficult relationships between certain of the countries from which the members came. I am sure that the more one gets to know people on a personal level the less chance there is of warfare between their respective countries.

The next PALS meeting was in Luxembourg. Regrettably I did not attend it. The curse on the German air stewardess therefore remained in abeyance.

The October 1978 meeting was in Amsterdam and this I did attend. Amsterdam is a fine city and, although I had been there before, this time it was a great advantage being shown around it by local people. Once again I was amazed at how many young people travelled around the city on bikes, the girlfriend often precariously perched on the crossbar of her boyfriend's bike. On our social day we visited a museum that was, I believe, just outside Delft. It was dedicated to Van Gogh paintings and had some early sketches that I had not seen before. These were realistic depictions of ordinary people and were in quite a different style to his later paintings.

Zurich in May 1981 was the next PALS meeting that I recall attending. At the time cross border mergers between law firms were regularly taking place in Europe and when this happened to a member of PALS it inevitably caused problems, because the other firm in the merger would most likely have different legal contacts in the same European cities. At this meeting the Dutch law firm informed us that they had just become associated with the English law firm Clifford Turner (later becoming by merger part of Clifford Chance) and that Clifford Turner already had its own offices in Paris, Brussels, Madrid etc. As a result of this it was decided to find another Dutch law firm to join the association, but meanwhile the two Dutch lawyers present agreed to remain as members. In fact we never did find another Dutch firm to join PALS and one of the Dutch lawyers (the one who knew his Shakespeare) continued to come to meetings for as long as I did. I believe that the PALS members continued to refer business to the Dutch law firm, but of course there was little chance of reciprocation.

On the Saturday our Swiss hosts took us by coach to Lucerne. It was, I remember clearly, a beautiful sunny day and the mountains surrounding Lucerne were covered with glistening snow. Lucerne shimmered in the sunshine - a most attractive place.

We went to Paris in May 1983. The meeting was memorable for a meal in a restaurant where every course had some part of a goose as its main ingredient. Also memorable was a visit to the magnificent chateau at Fontainebleau, the home of many French kings and some of their mistresses. Napoleon had also stayed there and left Fontainebleau to go into abdication in 1814. It was truly a most beautiful building and a great place to visit.

In November 1984 PALS came to London again, but I was not an official delegate for my firm, although I did attend part of the Friday working session and assisted with the entertainment.

In May 1985 there was a PALS meeting in Copenhagen which I did not attend. However, despite my absence, I was appointed to sit on a sub-committee with three colleagues to consider the possibility of joint ventures in the United States, South America, Africa, China or elsewhere. The sub-committee then met in Brussels in September 1985 and as the only member of the sub-committee with English as a first language I took the role of secretary and prepared the minutes of that meeting.

The next PALS meeting was in Milan in November 1985 and I naturally attended so that I could report to the members on the meeting of our sub-committee. From then on I became the unofficial secretary of PALS (this was made official in November 1990) and with one exception I attended all of the PALS meetings until my retirement as a solicitor.

Disregarding my attendances at the London meetings, I twice attended meetings in Amsterdam, Copenhagen, Madrid, Milan, Oslo, Paris and Zurich; and once in Athens, Barcelona, Berlin, Budapest, Brussels, Evora, Frankfurt, The Hague, Helsinki, Lisbon, Luxembourg, Stockholm and Vienna. Overall this was a pretty good clutch of European cities to visit at no cost to me. I should though add that, although very enjoyable, it was also pretty hard work, particularly after I took on the secretary's duties and became more involved in the running of the six-monthly meetings.

Like most associations (e.g. the European Union) PALS as it grew had a tendency to become more and more structured. After the brochure, more accurately called a directory, came a newsletter which I edited (what a formidable task it was to get any contributions). It did not last long. Then there were suggestions that we should have a written constitution. One of the main problems, though, was that some members wanted to promote PALS and their own law firm as a member of the association, whereas others were afraid of losing work by following the same course. Their worry was that law firms who were not members of PALS might well suspect that if they passed PALS' members any work there would likely be no reciprocation and accordingly they would refer work to a law firm with no such alliances. These underlying concerns accordingly made any type of joint venture very difficult to get off the ground.

Over time a few of the law firms resigned as members of PALS, usually because of conflicting loyalties, and on occasion new law firms joined the association, such as law firms from Dublin and Barcelona.

One topic that regularly turned up for discussion was the name of the association. Some members felt that PALS did not sound professional enough. The following acronyms were accordingly put forward at different times: ABLE, APLE, ELA, JUSTIN, PAEL and TEL. I personally felt that PALS was too low key and thought that ABLE, which I suggested and stood for Association of Business Lawyers in Europe was a better name. There was though amongst the members an attachment to the name PALS and some disagreement as to what to replace it with. PALS therefore remained the name of the association until after I retired when the name was indeed changed.

I usually found the business meetings very interesting and it was enlightening to discover how law firms in other European countries coped with the same sort of problems that faced English lawyers. However the real joy was to have direct conversations with the lawyers and their wives (or in one case husband) on the social days or over meals. These conversations were not necessarily about legal matters; indeed more commonly they were about the European lawyers' lives and interests and how they balanced their legal lives and their social lives. In this connection I never ceased to marvel at the ability of my European colleagues to switch from one language to another with ease. The Scandinavians I believe spoke their own language to each other so that a Dane would talk in Danish to a Swede who would reply in Swedish just as a Spaniard would speak in Spanish to a Portuguese who would reply in his own language. We may have started as PALS but in due course we did indeed become pals.

The one PALS meeting that I missed in the last 12 years of my involvement was the one in Zurich in September 1995.

This was a particularly important meeting for us because the London office of my firm had just merged with Bircham & Co, a law firm practising in Victoria near St James's Park station, and I was to introduce three partners from that practice to the various members of PALS. Our Ashford practice and later the Chislehurst practice had previously been transferred to the resident partners and the Croydon and Saffron Walden offices had become virtually independent. The London office standing alone was, I and my partners felt, now too small for the current marketplace and thus a merger with a larger practice was, we felt, the right step to take to safeguard our future.

Diverting from matters relating to PALS for a moment, I recall just before the merger speaking with a number of my partners about the name of the new practice. I said that it was a pity if our firm name was to disappear completely. I added that it would be rather nice if the merged practice could be called Bircham, Stoneham. One of my partners with a quick wit retorted with "Why not go the whole hog and call the new firm Bircham, Stoneham and Hangem!" In fact Bircham & Co remained the name of the merged practice and I was a litigation partner with that firm for the next two and a half years until, having reached my contractual retirement age, I retired at the somewhat early age of 62. I had accordingly stayed with the same firm from the moment I qualified to the moment I retired, albeit undergoing various mergers along the way.

Returning to my missed meeting, the reason I could not go to the Zurich meeting was that I had recently torn my Achilles tendon. I was on a fortnight's holiday with my wife and some friends in Thassos, a beautiful Greek island. Half way through our stay we went out to a restaurant one evening and had an excellent meal in the open air. It was a warm evening and the party was merry. The restaurant had a small band playing

Greek music and when one of my favourite songs was played I decided to get up and dance. Nobody would join me so I did my Greek dance, as indeed many of the Greek men do, on my own. A woman crossing the dance floor area came quite close to me and as she passed I heard a sound like a pistol shot. My right leg felt as if it had been kicked hard. I limped back to the table and told my wife and friends that the lady passing by me had kicked me in the leg – a somewhat unlikely scenario now that I look back on it. One of my friends who was a psychiatrist and had therefore undergone medical training had however heard the "shot" and said that it was much more likely that my Achilles had ruptured. My friend was unfortunately right and for a week I had to hobble around with the aid of a stick and to cadge lifts to and from the nearby beach.

When I got home from Thassos I thought that I had better check my condition out with my doctor. For some reason, and despite the diagnosis of my medical friend, I was convinced that it was just a turned ankle, but before I knew what was happening I was having a plaster cast put on my leg and being told that it would be inadvisable to fly to Zurich the next day. I was given some crutches and I staggered home somewhat late and told my wife the bad news. Unbeknown to me my wife was also having problems with her health. During the day my wife had been given some powerful eye drops and had been advised that she should not fly the following day. This accordingly answered the question I had been putting to myself, namely whether I should travel crutches notwithstanding. With my wife's support I may have ventured forth, but on my own this I think would have been foolhardy. Fortunately I was able to reach one of my new partners on the phone and tell him that I could not make it and that he and his two colleagues would have to introduce themselves to the other PALS members without my help. I am sure that my new partners managed all right without me, but I did feel that I had let them down.

The incident I have described was not the first time that I had hurt myself dancing or indeed had damaged my leg. Some years before Thassos I spent a holiday on the island of Kos in Greece One evening I was in an open air restaurant with friends. At the time a series of records had just come out called "Hooked on Classics." These were classical pieces that were jazzed up. One of my favourites was Beethoven's Fifth symphony which the restaurant band happened to play. I took hold of my partner and started dancing. At the back of the dance floor were about eight white steps and a platform. It looked a bit like a backdrop for an under-financed Fred Astaire movie. When the band played the easily recognisable series of notes that sound like "da da di da" repeated twice with heavy emphasis I could not resist dancing up each of the steps in time to the music and jumping off the platform. I landed on the beat, caught my somewhat astonished partner and carried on dancing. I may have impressed my partner, but my body was pressed rather than impressed and shortly after I felt sharp pains in my back where I had jarred the spine. It took me a number of weeks to recover, but, although I was often in pain, I was able to cope. I found when walking that the most comfortable position was to stride along with my right arm stretched upwards. I could not do this continuously though as people in the street might understandably have been worried about my mental state, but I did do it occasionally to get relief. Unfortunately when I did so I attracted taxi drivers who having stopped were not pleased when I told them that I was just stretching my arm and did not want a taxi at all.

The previous time that I broke my leg was in the late sixties when I was on a skiing trip in Ischgl in Austria with a party of about 30 people. I was a beginner and halfway through the fortnight our instructor thought that we were capable enough to ski down the mountain on our own. He was wrong! Roughly half way down I came to a section which in the summer was probably a road. On the left was a wall of snow and on the right was a drop down to a forest of firs. The trees were spread out and in to my mind came a scene from the film "The Pink Panther." In that scene David Niven is skiing towards a fir tree and then you lose sight of him and the next thing you see are the ski tracks, one on either side of the fir tree. Thinking of this I decided to keep to the left and in doing so hit a hard block of snow. Unfortunately my skis which were the old lengthy type did not release and the left one dug into the snow whilst my right leg carried on moving. Something had to give - and it was me. It hurt and I screamed with the pain. Fortunately this only lasted a few seconds. Other skiers from our party then arrived and in due course I was taken down the mountain on a stretcher. That was itself a thrilling experience as you are so close to the ground that the snow appears to rush past at enormous speed.

When I got back to the chalet where we were staying I had to wait to get a lift to the doctor who was in a nearby village. Whilst waiting one of my friends who did not know of my accident came down from the slopes and said until then he had never believed in werewolves, but that at exactly three o clock he had heard an unearthly scream coming from further up the mountain. I explained that I was his werewolf.

After a short wait I was taken to the village of Galtur where the nearest doctor was. I explained to the doctor who did not speak English that I could move my foot this way, that way and this way. He replied in German and I gathered that he was informing me that one of the ways was not possible. Not good news. The doctor's nurse then came into the surgery. She was a very pretty blonde girl who looked remarkably like Marilyn Monroe. The doctor said something to her in German which I did not understand and then they both took hold of my left leg and pulled hard. It hurt - and it did not work. The doctor then said something else to his nurse and she went off and came back with a gun which she handed to him. I know in England we shoot lame racehorses, but I hoped in Austria that they did not shoot lame skiers. The doctor then pointed at the gun and said "eezer eezer." He then demonstrated by putting the gun in his mouth and pulling the trigger. I felt as if I was playing a part in some bizarre film. I then realised that the doctor was trying to explain that the gun contained ether and I was to provide my own anaesthesia. It was a clever device because as you started to pass out you naturally stopped pulling the trigger. It is strange because, even though I now knew what was going on, it still felt very uncomfortable to put a gun in my mouth and pull the trigger. As I was losing consciousness the doctor said "was ist ihr name?" I presume he was checking to make sure I was sedated. I looked at the nurse and thought it would be very funny to say "Marilyn Monroe", but the ether seemed to work as a truth drug and try as I did the words would not come. Somewhat feebly I gave my own name. "Mehr eezer, mehr eezer", the doctor responded. I dutifully complied and this time I passed out and the doctor and nurse were able to have another tug of war with my leg - this time with success. A heavy plaster was then put on my leg and I was driven back to my chalet.

For the second week of my holiday I traded in my skis for a sledge and I was lucky enough to find somebody in the party each day to pull me out to the nursery slopes. Their return for this service was the chance to play a game which amused them and terrified me. My "carer" would drag me to the top of the nursery slopes whereupon he would point the sledge and in particular my plastered foot at the open gate at the bottom of the slopes and then let the sledge go. The object of the game was to ski after me and try to stop the sledge before it went through the gap or crashed into the adjoining walls.

On my return to England I went to St. Bartholomew's Hospital for the cast to be looked at. Two young doctors saw me in a curtained cubicle outside of which was a queue of patients waiting to be seen. One doctor said to the other with reference to my cast "I think we will have to take it off." The other replied "We shall need to use the saw." One of them then went off and returned with the saw and started sawing away, making the sounds a saw does make. The heavy cast eventually fell away and a light one was put on instead. As I left the cubicle though I noticed most of the remaining patients in the queue looked distinctly green!

Having digressed, back to PALS. Being part of this association for so many years has left me with many happy memories of my PALS trips and I shall now recount a few that I particularly recall.

When visiting Amsterdam I remember going on to see Haarlem in the centre of the tulip bulb growing area. It was a very attractive place, but as we were walking around the city it started to pour with rain. Nobody seemed to be carrying umbrellas so we all went into a small shop and almost cleared them out of portable umbrellas. I have, looking back, a mental image of the PALS members strolling around Haarlem under the shelter of pink umbrellas. I suspect though that the colour of the umbrellas may be a figment of my imagination.

On one of the Copenhagen trips we had our formal Friday night dinner in a large aquarium. We ate surrounded by electric eels, fluorescent fish and sharks swimming around in their glass cages. I suppose some people might say that as lawyers we should have been quite at home eating with the sharks!

When in Madrid we went on to visit Segovia where there is a truly magnificent Roman aqueduct. It is amazing to think the

Romans started building this at the end of the first century A.D. It is also in Segovia that I ate suckling pig for the first time. On another visit to Madrid we went on to Aranjuez where there are beautiful green gardens - a real surprise in an otherwise desert landscape. I also recall on this occasion persuading my somewhat reluctant Bircham partners to go to a flamenco show one evening in a Madrid restaurant. Flamenco is a type of dancing I particularly enjoy and I did not wish to miss the chance. The dancers were a very athletic young man and a very pretty young woman. We were some way back, but a group of Chinese tourists who were sitting at the very front left and we took their places. The young woman was wearing a colourful tiered flamenco dress and as she spun round it became apparent that she was not wearing anything underneath it. I can see now the look of amazement on one of my partner's faces. In fact the young couple were both excellent flamenco dancers and we had a great evening.

Milan was memorable for the beautiful Cathedral (you can walk on the roof), the impressive railway station built by order of Mussolini, the enormous but beautiful arcades and "The Last Supper" painted on the wall of a convent refectory by Leonardo da Vinci. It was also memorable for two visits to La Scala, the opera house. On the first visit we heard "The Alpine symphony" by Richard Strauss and on the second a little known opera "Fedora" by Giordano. As tickets are not easy to come by this was on each occasion a great treat.

On the Oslo visits I recollect going out in the bay on a beautiful day in a motor vessel hired by our hosts. It was very relaxing and we had great views of the city and the nearby coastline. We also went to the top of the Oslo ski jump, apparently the site of the second oldest ski jump competition in the world. It was just under 200 feet high and standing at the top and looking down the run made me realise how brave those ski jumpers are. We also enjoyed a panoramic view of

116

Oslo. My wife and I later visited the Munch museum on the outskirts of Oslo to see in particular "The Scream" which had been fairly recently stolen and then fortunately recovered.

Zurich I remember for a visit into the countryside. We were in lush meadows with mountains as a backdrop. Our hosts explained that in the particular area it was considered very therapeutic to walk through the wet grass barefoot. We dutifully took off our socks, stockings and shoes and tramped through the grass. After a short hike we reached a nunnery and the nuns came out with small barrels filled with hot water and we sat down with our feet in the barrels - all part of the therapeutic process. I vividly recall our senior Dutch lawyer dressed in a dark suit with his trousers rolled up, his feet in the barrel, his back upright and his rolled umbrella clutched in his right hand. Where was my camera?

On our Athens visit we travelled on to Nafplion, the old capital of modern Greece situated in the Peloponnese. We stayed at a magnificent hotel built into rock. Our hosts had laid on a trip to Mycenae - on the Sunday I believe. I was looking forward to this because when I was very young I had seen a   picture of the famous Lion Gate in a book and vowed to see it for real one day. The coach came and it worked its way upwards out of Nafplion to the archaeological site. It was hot and sunny. We arrived and there was the site just behind the wall. It was guarded by armed men. My anticipation was great. Sadly my hopes were just about to be dashed. Mycenae was shut for the day! All the efforts of our hosts fell on deaf ears. They told the guards we were very important people and we should have a private view, but to no avail. One of our Danish lawyers who was young and fit saw a possible way in which required vaulting over a wire fence. He was all for it, but we dissuaded him and thereby saved his life or at least prevented a diplomatic incident. I suspect our poor hosts were mortified. Sadly at the time of writing I still have not returned to Mycenae.

We visited Berlin in May 1994. The Wall had been pulled down some four years earlier, but we saw the fragment that had been kept. The English party also got a taxi driver to take us to the spot where Hitler's bunker had been and where he had committed suicide. We asked why there was no plaque and the taxi driver explained that the authorities had forbidden any marking in case it became a shrine for Neo-Nazis. It was a quiet spot and I later wondered if the taxi driver knew anything more than us. I suspect that foreign visitors regularly made this request and that taxi drivers took them somewhere quiet and all parties were duly satisfied.

Budapest was a particularly special venue for our PALS meeting in October 1989. The country was shaking off its communist past and the red stars which dotted the city were being taken down. Indeed Hungary became a republic that very month. What timing on the part of our Austrian hosts. I will not easily forget our day out on this trip. We went to a town whose name I cannot now recall and if I could I would likely not be able to spell. It was apparently famous for the fact that almost every house chimney had a nest of storks at its top. Its fame was well merited and the sight of these large birds flying in to and out of their nests was amazing. After our coach parked we explored and then we all went into a restaurant for morning coffee. We were told to reassemble at eleven thirty. The coffee was particularly good and my wife decided to have a second cup. I said we did not have time, but she said that the coach would not leave without us. She was wrong! When we reached the place where the coach had been there was an empty space. The street was deserted and I did not know where we were going next. Not surprisingly I did not speak Hungarian, but more significantly I had very little Hungarian currency. After walking a short way we came to

118

the Mayor's house which doubled up as the tourist office. We went in and fortunately found someone who spoke English. We were told that there was no taxi service in the town and that if we wanted a taxi one would have to come from Budapest which was some 30 to 40 miles away. The tourist officer then suggested that before committing ourselves we should walk around the town in case our colleagues had stopped somewhere else. As the town was not large and the coach had left a perfectly good parking spot this seemed to me very unlikely. Nevertheless off we went. The streets were still very quiet. As we went down a hill though we heard sounds of laughter and chatter coming from behind a closed door. We went in and found our colleagues engaged in a wine tasting. I was extremely glad to see them, but a little miffed that we had not been missed.

On the Saturday evening we went to the Opera House and saw a fine production of "Lucia di Lammermoor" by Donizetti. The building was very ornate, having recently been restored. I particularly remember going into the grand bar in the interval and having a glass of champagne which cost under fifty pence. It was not very good, but at that price one could not expect better. Overall this was a memorable weekend.

On our visit to Frankfurt our hosts took us to Heidelberg (home of "The Student Prince" and duelling clubs). We went around the castle which looks down on the town and I recalled an earlier visit when I was travelling on my own. On that occasion I was taken around the castle on a guided tour, the party consisting of about 20 or so women and me. The ladies were wives of American servicemen stationed nearby and at the end we all had our photograph taken. I wonder if their husbands later asked them who the solitary guy in the photograph was. "Just some Limey" they probably replied.

The Hague visit I recall because we stayed in the magnificent Hotel des Indes. The hotel was renowned for the famous people who had stayed there. These included Mata Hari, the spy and Anna Pavlova, the dancer. Indeed Pavlova died in the hotel and there was a suite named in her honour. I thought that the owners had to be pretty confidant of their hotel's reputation to name a suite after a guest who had actually passed away whilst staying at their hotel. Perhaps though less knowledgeable guests thought that the suite was named in honour of a meringue!

Our Portuguese hosts took us to Sintra, the town of palaces on the hill, much praised by Lord Byron and deservedly so. For me the other highlight was going to a good restaurant and listening to fado, the mournful songs sung with heart-breaking emotion by - in my experience - rather plain middle aged Portuguese ladies.

When we were in Luxembourg we went by coach to a small village on the river Moselle. We were taken by our hosts around a small vineyard that they partly owned and then on to a building which was the place where a secret wine society met. Our hosts were themselves members of this club and as an extraordinary measure were prepared to enrol their fellow lawyers from abroad. To test whether we were suitable we were blindfolded and asked to identify a particular wine. "Riesling" I said when it was my turn. I was right. It was not difficult though because as far as I could tell that was the only local grape variety. I and the other lawyers then had to kneel whilst one of our hosts tapped each of us on each shoulder with a sword. Some special words were spoken and we were then given our insignia as new members. Sadly I have never attended any further meeting of this excellent society.

I only visited Vienna once and apart from finding it a fine city my main recollection is of being entertained by one of my firm's clients who lived there on the Saturday evening. He took the English party of four (two lawyers and two wives) to the Hotel Sacher for an excellent meal finished off with their famous sachertorte (a chocolate cake with whipped cream). We then went to the opera house - and what were they staging but "Lucia di Lammermoor." Afterwards we went to a sort of restaurant where they had a sizeable dance floor. The dances were traditional ballroom dances with, of course, the Viennese waltz added. An enjoyable and varied evening. The next day I was determined to go on Vienna's Big Wheel, made famous in the film "The Third Man." My companions were reluctant, but I persisted and up we went. As I suffer from vertigo though I was not tempted to emulate Orson Welles and open the door at the top of the wheel's run. Despite my problem with heights it was well worth it. In fact, having got the party in an adventurous mood, I followed up with getting them to go for a ride on a roller coaster/water splash which was nearby.

The PALS meeting in London in October 1994 was an important one for two reasons. First it was the twentieth anniversary meeting and secondly my wife and I with some help were organising it. We decided to book the visitors into Brown's hotel in Mayfair as we thought they might like a traditional English hotel rather than one in a chain. The hotel looked after everybody very well and I think that it was a good choice. On the Friday evening I gave the speech traditionally made by a member of the host firm and on the Saturday we took our guests to Blenheim Palace. This was a great success as there was a Churchill exhibition on which was of real interest to a number of our colleagues. It was fascinating to see the French and German delegates discussing the exhibits together. Lunch was in a restaurant in nearby Woodstock. This was very good, but at some point we realised that two of our company were missing and we had to send out a search party as they did not know where we were lunching. Fortunately they were quickly found, happily strolling down the street apparently without a care in the world. Overall I think this was a successful and happy meeting, but it is certainly very tiring if you have to organise it yourselves.

My last PALS trip which was in October 1997 was to Evora, a world heritage site in the Alentejo district of Portugal. Evora has a Roman temple, Roman baths and used to have an important Jesuit university. A modern one was reopened in 1973. In the fifteenth century Evora was the residence of the Portuguese kings. A most beautiful place in which to make my farewell speech, which I think went down well. It was for me an emotional time as I had been closely connected with PALS for 23 years. On our social day we visited a quinta (historically a farm rented at one fifth of its income) that belonged to the family of one of the partners in the Lisbon office. Our hosts showed us how cork was collected from the trees for the making of bottle corks and other articles and we then had a splendid lunch in cool white painted buildings. The local wines we were served were also particularly good. As Stoneham & Sons had opened their Lisbon office in 1924 and thereby put down roots in mainland Europe Portugal was an appropriate place to bring my involvement with PALS to an end.

The formation and development of PALS was something in which I think I can justifiably take some pride. I learned a lot from my European colleagues and I went to some interesting places that I might not otherwise have ever visited. I made many new friends and I had many enjoyable experiences. I think my contact with lawyers from other countries also made me into a better lawyer. Going away for four days every six months to different European countries became a significant part of my business and personal life. Being the secretary of the association though meant that I had some responsibility for the success of each meeting and having to be generally available was somewhat tiring. I know that in the latter years my wife, although she enjoyed the PALS trips immensely, found them quite exhausting. My wife though had the advantage that English was her first language and I can hardly contemplate how tiring it must have been for those wives from abroad who did not speak English as well as their husbands. Now that I am retired I am particularly glad that the organisation, albeit under a different name, is still going strong. Long may it continue to grow and to prosper.

If any of my old friends who were members of PALS should chance to read these recollections they should know that I have very fond memories of all of them. It is, I believe, extraordinary to meet quite a large number of people from so many different countries and like and respect them all, but that is how it was. Seeing each other over three or four days every six months or so created a bond and I knew some of my colleagues in PALS better than some of my own partners.

CHAPTER SEVEN

South America

Stoneham & Sons had many contacts in South America, but by 1980 there was nobody in Stoneham Langton & Passmore who had met any of them personally. It was therefore decided that one of the partners should go around South America, visit existing contacts, make new ones and report back. Another partner was scheduled to go, but I think he was a little reluctant and I eagerly stepped into the breach as I had always wanted to visit South America. It became the only time in my career that I was away from my office desk for as long as a whole month.

The first thing I did by way of preparation was to list all the law firms I already knew of that I wished to visit. I then checked up on those firms in Martindale-Hubbell. This gave me the names of partners and other useful information. I then checked the same directory for major countries in South America where the firm had no established contacts and chose law firms that appeared potentially suitable. That gave me a working list. I then checked with our bankers to see who they would instruct in the various countries and I also found out which firms the local consulates would recommend. I then compiled my final list of law firms to which I added consulates and banks. My intention was to visit more than one law firm in each city and with banks and consulates to see as well I gave myself a pretty heavy itinerary. I also built in to the programme some places that I wanted to see simply as a tourist. After all I was going to be away for a whole month!

I left Heathrow at 8.30 p.m. on Friday 29 February 1980, arriving back in Heathrow about the same time on Sunday 30 March 1980. If I went into the office the next day, and I cannot now remember, I must have been quite exhausted.

My first destination was Rio de Janeiro in Brazil. I arrived in Rio at about 7 a.m. on Saturday 1 March 1980. On the flight I had chatted to a director of a large pharmaceutical company and as he had a driver meeting him at the airport he offered me a lift into town. I had read that Rio was a dangerous city and I asked the Brazilian driver if this was true "Well" he said "you could say so" and he went on to tell me of a recent experience when he had parked his car on the road adjoining Copacabana beach. The driver told me he went for a swim and then returned to his car and got in intending to drive home. He said that suddenly a man leant in through his side window, pointed a gun at him and asked for his keys. All this in broad daylight in a well populated part of the city. The driver refused and the gunman put a bullet just to the right of the driver's foot which was resting on the accelerator. "Give me the keys" the gunman said again. The driver refused. The gunman then put a bullet just to the left of the driver's foot and said "Next time centre." "What did you do?" I asked. "What do you think?" said the driver "I gave him the bloody keys." Whether telling this story distracted the driver I do not know, but he then drove the wrong way up a one way street and we were stopped by armed police. The director suggested that I slip away and I therefore exited the car swiftly and got a taxi the rest of the way. I hope my friends did not get into any real trouble, but I must say that armed police do look much more threatening than our unarmed coppers.

After resting in the morning I went out of my hotel in the afternoon for a walk along the side of some of Rio's fabulous beaches. Particularly noticeable were the large number of extremely attractive young men and women on the beaches and the paucity of their swimwear. This was before thongs had made their appearance on English beaches. I also took the cable car up to the top of Sugar Loaf mountain (the strangely shaped feature that stretches out into the bay) and imagined that I was James Bond being chased by Jaws in the film

"Moonraker." This was all very much in the mind though as there is no way that I would ever consider climbing out of a cable car whilst it was suspended in space. The view looking back at the rest of Rio from Sugar Loaf, as anybody who has been there will recall, is absolutely stunning. Surely one of the best city views in the world.

I think jet lag kicked in on the next day which was a Sunday and, after a lazy morning spent by the side of the hotel pool, I could only manage one tourist attraction. I had been warned by the hotel only to take official taxis as there were stories of unauthorised taxi drivers taking tourists into the hills, beating them up and and robbing them. I therefore ordered a taxi from the hotel and the driver took me on a tortuous ride to the top of Corcovado mountain. On top of this pinnacle stands the statue called "Christ the Redeemer." It is enormous - about 125 feet high standing on a peak which is over 2300 feet high. The view of Rio bay from the base of the statue is truly breathtaking. Sugar Loaf is directly in view and on a nice day - which it was when I was there - the edges of the whole bay were sharply defined. With the possible exception of Venice, Rio is the most beautiful city that I have ever visited.

On Monday it was back to work. I visited the British Consulate and then a firm which had longish connections with my firm. After lunching with two of the partners I visited another law firm in the afternoon. In travelling around Rio I was struck by the contrast between wealth and poverty. There are fine office buildings in the centre of the city, but not far away are the favelas, the slums in which the poor eke out a living. Walking was quite hazardous as many of the drain grills were missing and there were other signs of lack of attention to safety or possibly lack of money to put it right. I am of course describing Rio and the other places that I visited in South America as they were in 1980. Unfortunately I have never been back and thirty odd years later it could be a different story.

I went out to a restaurant that evening (much more interesting than staying in the hotel) and at this point perhaps I could mention Brazilian food. Any kind of steak, particularly with black bean sauce, was excellent. Also I particularly liked the fact that in most restaurants as soon as you sat down a waiter or waitress arrived with a plate with a spicy hot sausage or something similar on it so that you could nibble this whilst reading the menu. That evening before going to bed I turned the television on and was hooked by a film called "Hercules v Genghis Khan" in which all the actors spoke Portuguese. This must surely go down as one of my most memorable T.V. watching evenings ever.

On Tuesday I had more business appointments, but in between I was able to visit the church of Sao Francisco, an ornate baroque church with, it is said, more gold in it than any other church in the New World. The impact on entering such a building, and there are many such in South America, is overpowering. The shimmering gold which is all over the place is immensely impressive, whether you like it or not. Back at the hotel a Dutch lady told me a story of a man sitting in a bus with blood on his hands - the reason being that he was clutching two ladies fingers with the rings still on. I cannot vouch for the truth of this story, but it fits in with other cautionary tales that I heard.

On the hotel reception desk that day I saw a poster advertising a guided night tour of Rio. I signed up for it thinking I might meet some more English speaking travellers. I had had no difficulty with the people that I met on business who all spoke excellent English, but the average Brazilian was unlikely to speak English and there seemed to be no English guests in my hotel. The poster promised amongst other things a samba club and a macumba ritual - an African based religious ceremony with links to witchcraft. I was the only person from my hotel going and so I waited for what turned out to be a minibus. Apart from the driver there was Pancho the Brazilian guide and eight Argentines. Not what I had expected. However one of the Argentines, a young lady, spoke some English and I was put in her charge. The first thing Pancho then told us was that macumba was off. This was a disappointment, but nothing could be done about it. I do not suppose that I will ever attend a macumba ceremony now! The first stop was to visit Corcovado. Although I had already been there it is difficult to say whether the view was better by day or by night. It was certainly extremely beautiful. We then went to a Brazilian steak house and had a typical Brazilian meal. Afterwards the party went to a nightclub called "The Katakombe." This specialised in samba dancing and we were entertained by some extremely attractive samba dancers who wore costumes that were smaller than bikinis. Once the show was over all could join in and dance the samba. I danced with my Argentine companion and a number of other ladies. One, whom I later found out taught samba, danced with me for a while. She then asked me in Portuguese whether I was Argentinian. I realised what she meant and I said no. She then asked me whether I was Brazilian and I again said no. "Ingles" I said. She looked astonished and I have always since liked to believe that she was amazed that an Englishman could dance the samba so well. There is probably a totally different explanation, but it is pleasant to have such delusions. Despite the lack of macumba it was a memorable evening.

More business on Wednesday morning. In the afternoon I visited Copacabana and Ipanema beaches, two of the most famous beaches in the world. Ipanema is well known through the song "The Girl from Ipanema" and Copacabana is well known as one of the best beaches in the world. The beaches were full of very fit young people playing beach football, volleyball and other such games and what particularly struck me, as it had done on the earlier day, was how good looking they all were. I wondered if people living in Rio who were ordinary looking were too embarrassed to visit the beaches. On my return to the hotel I got talking to an English geologist who had just returned from working in the jungle. I asked him how dangerous it was there and he told me of a recent occasion when the group he was in had set up camp and he had gone off to explore the terrain. The geologist told me that he was away some hours and when he returned he was horrified to find that the local Indians, who did not like intruders, had massacred his colleagues and left them lying around with arrows sticking out of their now lifeless bodies. I have no reason to doubt this story and I considered the geologist to be a brave man to carry on after such an experience. For me though it was early to bed as I was off to Sao Paulo the next day.

On Thursday I flew in to Sao Paulo, then one of the largest cities in the world. I had to rush from the hotel for my first appointment which was with two partners in the same law firm that I had visited at the beginning of my stay in Rio. We happened to discuss billing practices and they told me that they had to send bills to clients once a fortnight because of monthly devaluation! After lunch I saw a banker and another couple of lawyers who took me out to dinner which, although the food was very good, was memorable because of a tropical storm which flooded the streets in minutes. It is the only time in my life that I have seen a car floating down a road. My hosts then drove me around Sao Paulo and I was impressed by the number of fine large buildings. I was less impressed by the traffic which was horrendous. I believe at that time Sao Paulo had the worst reputation in the world for traffic jams.

Friday was very much a working day. First a banker, then the consul general, then the chairman of the chamber of commerce and then to a lawyer whose offices were in his home, a beautiful house in a residential area. The entire length of one side of his offices was covered with glass through which one could see the lush greenery outside. This particular lawyer was educated in Crediton, Devon and because of this background had a number of English connections already. Finally to another law firm who I suspect did little international work. A busy and tiring day.

On Saturday I had a day off business. I first went to the Butanta Institute a place where they study poisonous snakes. I found it a little disappointing so I decided to go on and visit the zoo. The taxi took forever. There was a traffic gridlock and the taxi driver did not know where the zoo was or where my hotel was either. Eventually we arrived at the zoo. It was a fine zoo, but everything was very spread out and there was a lot of walking to be done. Later I dined out with one of my legal contacts and his wife and on my return to my hotel I heard the sound of a gunshot shortly after followed by the sound of an ambulance. My overall impression of Sao Paulo was a city with too many cars and too many people, albeit very friendly.

On Sunday I was due to fly to Montevideo in Uruguay. What I thought to myself do I know of Uruguay. Their football team won the first World Cup, Fray Bentos who made corned beef packed in tins which was very popular during the war was in Uruguay and the capital Montevideo was on the River Plate. That was about it. Later I discovered that Montevideo was occupied by the British for just over six months in 1807. In any event I was looking forward to seeing a country I would probably never visit on holiday.

When I arrived in Montevideo I found it sleepy compared with the Brazilian cities I had visited. It had though a quiet charm of its own. I walked to the port and was surprised to find that the River Plate was so wide that one could not see Buenos Aires or indeed any part of Argentina which lay on the other side. For my evening meal I just had to have steak and I am pleased to say it compared favourably with the steak in Brazil.

On Monday I visited our Embassy and then took the most battered taxi I have ever travelled in. The driver looked like "Desperate Dan" from "The Dandy" comic, having two or three days bristle and sporting a very hairy chest to match. The taxi had what looked like, and in the circumstances I believe could have been, two bullet holes in the windscreen and its top speed with the foot pressed hard down was just over 30 miles per hour. I called on a lawyer and then a banker who told me that the British used to have a substantial presence in Uruguay and Argentina, particularly in communications, but that the Germans had now taken over. I then visited another banker and after him a representative of the chamber of commerce. By now I was pretty tired. It is exhausting seeing one new person after another, however interesting they might be so I went back to the hotel and had a nap, followed by dinner and a tango show. Tango, as in Argentina, is very popular in Uruguay. The show was very good and as well as the dancing I particularly enjoyed some very dramatic singing by two men and an attractive girl wearing a bright red dress.

On Tuesday I had a free morning and I wandered around Montevideo, noting how new buildings had sprung up next to old ones. I met a businessman and his wife for lunch at his golf club. My host told me that cars in Uruguay cost between five to ten times U.K. prices - perhaps this explains why my earlier taxi driver had not upgraded his vehicle!

In the afternoon I flew to Buenos Aires, the capital of Argentina and a very fine city. After standing in a queue to

131

book in at the Sheraton and unpacking I went out to a restaurant in a street called Lavalle (another steak). This particular street had more cinemas in it than I have ever seen anywhere else. Buenos Aires is built to a large extent on a grid pattern and has boulevards with pavement cafes that reminded me of Paris. After the dangers of the streets of Rio it was noticeable how many young men and young girls, often unaccompanied, walked freely about Buenos Aires even after dark. I later discovered that this was due to a regime that operated a policy of zero tolerance. I heard that pickpockets had their fingers amputated. The young women, sometimes accompanied sometimes alone, who were walking along the pavements from café to café were mostly very attractive. I thought the same in Rio and I came to the conclusion that it was due in a large part to their posture. It was as if every young woman was imagining herself to be on a catwalk. The city had a very pleasant feel to it - indeed there was only one thing I did not like about Buenos Aires and that was the rampant inflation (at the time one British pound was worth approximately 3800 pesos).

On Wednesday I got up and went down for breakfast, but there was another queue so I had to skip my first meal of the day. I walked to the chamber of commerce and saw one of their representatives. On to see a banker and then I got somewhat lost looking for a particular law firm, which turned out to be the largest law firm in Argentina with about forty lawyers. The partner I saw told me that there was always a secretary available as they worked two shifts covering a 12 hour period, which was an interesting, albeit to me unwelcome, idea. I then went on to call on two more law firms. The first appointment overrun, but I was I thought just in time for the second appointment. What I had not bargained for was that the offices would be on the eighth floor and the lift would be broken. I do not like being late so I ran up the stairs and arrived at the top panting for breath. The receptionist showed me straight in and it was clear that the partner I was to see had forgotten who I was. "Where have you come from?" he said. "London" I gasped. "Did you run all the way?" was his reply. Later in the afternoon I managed to get in a swim in the hotel pool which was very refreshing and after eating out I had a few very expensive beers in the hotel bar. So far I am not at all impressed by the Sheraton.

On Thursday I managed to get breakfast at the hotel. I then went on to the British Embassy and a bank. Next I saw two partners in a law firm with whom I had had dealings in my London office. After I had looked around their offices, the two partners took me to lunch at their club. After lunch I saw another lawyer who told me that he had played cricket for Argentina. I did not tell him that I did not know that Argentina played cricket. Finally I attended my last appointment - with yet another lawyer. By now I was ready for an early night, but one of the partners in one of the firms that I had visited during the day had invited me for dinner at his parents' apartment so it was another late night.

On Friday because of the queue I again skipped breakfast (this is not a good idea) and went to see a lawyer who had been awarded the OBE - a very nice man. I then had some free time so I went to have a look at the Casa Rosada, the presidential palace from which Eva Peron rallied her supporters and the Cathedral which looks very like the British Museum from the outside. Lunch was a particular pleasure because I met up with the brother of one of my partners and I could relax. My mixed grill was so large that I took a photograph of it as a memento. Back at the Sheraton I tried to ring home, but after two fruitless hours I gave up and went for a swim instead. In the evening I had been invited to have dinner at the house of one of the lawyers I had met the day before. When I arrived I was introduced to the lawyer's wife and was interested to discover that she had been a Miss

Duncan before marriage. We sat at a large dining table in a beautiful dining room with a French tapestry on the wall. A maid served us with soup and then a fish pie. It was very formal, but also very pleasant.

Back at the hotel I got into conversation with a lady who was a Canadian lawyer and her male companion. She told me that they had just come from the Iguassu Falls (one of the largest waterfalls in the world and featured in the film "The Mission"). I told them that I was very envious of them as I had wanted to see the Iguassu Falls, but could not fit it into my itinerary. It was my last night at the Sheraton, a frustrating hotel where one waits for the lifts, for one's keys, for breakfast and of course to book out.

On Saturday I flew to the other side of South America, namely to Lima the capital of Peru. The flight took over four hours, but it was not boring and there were times when I had a really good view of the Andes. On approaching the airport the plane went very close to a mountain, but after landing at Rio - a similar experience - I was hardened to such dangers. Peru is a fascinating country, but Lima itself was somewhat scruffy. The hotel I stayed in, The Crillon, was a very nice hotel and a contrast to the somewhat characterless Sheraton. Unfortunately I soon discovered that the days of large and tasty steaks were behind me. Meat was scarce in Peru and there were days in the week when it was not permitted to have meat on the menu. At the top of the hotel was an excellent dining room/night club called The Sky Room which I visited that evening. Every night Peruvian dancers would put on a display of folk dances. The dancers wore colourful costumes and they were accompanied by a band playing distinctive local music. I did not then enquire, but I now believe that the band played the charango (a type of mandolin), the siku (panpipes), the cajon (a box with a hole in it) and the tarka (a sort of flute). In any event the music was hypnotic. I especially liked the reedy sound and watching the musician whose job it was to slap the box with his hands. All told a good start to my visit to the Western countries in South America.

Although I had business appointments in Peru I had built in to my itinerary a trip to Cusco and Machupicchu, places I was very keen to visit. When I arrived at Lima airport on the Sunday I found that there was a mix up with my reservation, but fortunately there was one seat available and off I flew to Cusco. Cusco was the capital of the Inca empire and is about 11000 feet above sea level - in fact the highest I had ever been. When I got out of the plane I felt a little wobbly due to altitude sickness. Arriving at the hotel I was promptly greeted with a cup of coca tea which is a well-established remedy for such a condition. Sadly in my case it was not fully effective, because I had a dull headache throughout my stay in Cusco. Hotel Monasterio was absolutely charming. It was originally built in 1595 and rebuilt after serious damage from an earthquake in 1650. It had been a university and a seminary until in 1965 it became a hotel. It has a very fine central courtyard with a cedar tree reputedly over 250 years old and a fountain and this was surrounded by stone cloisters with balconies above. It was a very peaceful place to stay in.

Following advice I took an afternoon sleep to try and shake off the altitude sickness and I then went out to explore. There is a large central square in Cusco where I photographed some Indians who had come into town to sell their colourful fabrics. They were cooking soup in the street whilst their llamas watched with interest. Back at the hotel I had dinner serenaded by Peruvian musicians. I am really getting into this South American music!

The train to Machupicchu left Cusco at 7 a.m. on Monday morning and the journey took four hours. The start of the journey is a steep climb out of Cusco and I was relaxing and looking back at the city when the train came to a stop and then it started to reverse back towards Cusco. "Oh dear" I thought "something has gone wrong and I will never get to Machupicchu after all." Suddenly the train stopped and went forward again. This procedure was repeated a number of times and I realised that the gradient was so steep that the train was zig-zagging its way over the mountains. I believe this is a fairly rare technique, but I wished somebody had told me what would happen in advance. One of my partners who is a railway buff I am sure would have known all about it.

The railway follows the sacred river of the Incas latterly called the Urubamba and it is an interesting journey with views of the Andes and when passing through villages sights of the local people in their colourful outfits, the women wearing bowler hats, trilbys or other unusual headgear. The Indian children were particularly keen to see the train, although it must have been a regular sight, and they would run out of their houses and wave. It reminded me of my childhood when I would do the same when the steam train went by. Finally the train arrived and I joined a long queue for coaches up a corkscrew road.

In my experience where one's expectation is high disappointment usually follows. However there are some places where the reverse is the case, such as the Taj Mahal, Rio and Venice to which I can now add Machupicchu. It is breath-taking, both literally and metaphorically. Although it looks much higher than Cusco it is in fact about 3000 feet lower and miraculously my headache completely disappeared. There were few tourists compared to the size of the site and I walked around the houses, some of which had restored thatched roofs, bumping into llamas and alpacas who appeared to be touring as well. The site of the ruins with the conical mountains as a backdrop was as good as the travel posters (not always the case) and I was blessed with a beautiful warm and sunny day. In fact climbing the many steps made me quite hot. After a while I noted three boisterous children who were clambering on the walls at the edge of the site irrespective of the precipitous drops to the jungle below. I then got talking to their parents who were also staying at my hotel in Cusco. The husband had been the manager of a bank in Sao Paulo that I had in fact visited and, his stint being up, he was on his way home to England. When I came to take the coach from the site down to the railway station I noticed that a number of young Indian boys aged about 10 or so would approach the coaches, smile at the passengers and then race the coaches to the bottom. However whereas the coaches would zig-zag down the road the youngsters would go in a direct line helter-skelter over grassy hummocks or whatever other obstacle was in their way. When my coach arrived at the end of the road there was one of the young Indian boys, sweating profusely with his hand held out. I reckon that he fully deserved the few coins he collected to which I made a substantial contribution.

The return train journey seemed very long and at one point I got cramp in my leg which shot up in the air knocking over the trestle table on which my camera was resting. I did not know it at the time but the camera was damaged and all subsequent photographs came out totally black - what a disappointment I had when I later viewed my prints. On return to my hotel I found it almost completely deserted so I went to bed early after a long but highly satisfying day.

Tuesday was destined to be a day of religion. First I visited the Church of La Merced which had the most beautiful cloisters - a place of quiet meditation. Then I revisited the main square called the Plaza de Armas. This is a key selling area for the Indians and I was regularly chased by Indian women trying to sell their wares. The women had very wide hips and low centres of gravity and on their backs they normally carried bundles of something or other and sometimes babies. The women nearly all wore bowler hats whereas the men wore a sort of nightcap with big earflaps. I bought a multi-coloured Indian belt as a present for one of my children. The square was full of activity. There were shoeshine men, magazine stalls and other diversions. Turning back to my religious quest I visited the Cathedral of Santo Domingo which had unusually a solid silver altar. Then on to the Church of La Compania de Jesus which had a magnificent gilded altar. I returned to my hotel for lunch and then went on to the Church of San Blas which had a beautifully carved wooden pulpit. Next was the Museum of Religious Art which is housed in the Archbishop's Palace, a simple but attractive building. Inside were religious paintings and a charming courtyard. Santa Catalina was the last church of the day. It was quite dark by now and an old man who I presumed was the caretaker took me around the church and turned the lights on as we went. Another fine altarpiece of gilded cedar - indeed there were four more gilded altarpieces as well.

After so much ancient art I thought that it would be a nice contrast to finish the day with some modern art, but that museum was closed. Perhaps it was just as well as I had probably seen enough for one day. My overall impression of the churches in Cusco was how elaborately and sumptuously they were decorated: the fact that most surfaces were covered in gold leaf was very impressive, but it was also somewhat suffocating.

On the way back to my hotel I saw an Indian woman sitting on the pavement breastfeeding her baby as if it was perfectly normal, which of course it really is. That evening I dined at the hotel where I met up with the banker and his family that I had talked to at Machupicchu. The banker told me that he was returning to England to work in the bank's head office in London and that he would be looking for somewhere to live; he then asked me where I lived and I told him that I had a house in a place called Radlett in Hertfordshire. I must have extolled the virtues of Radlett because I later discovered that the banker and his family bought a house there - ironically I had by then moved elsewhere. Later I went to the hotel bar for a drink, but it was virtually empty. I suspect that everybody in this hotel goes to bed early because they are either just about to make an early start on their way to Machupicchu or having been there are exhausted the next day. A lovely hotel, but I could have done with a little more life in the evenings. I was also missing the Peruvian music and dance. I did not visit any law firms in Cusco, the reader will have noticed, as I saw no possibility of work there for an English lawyer - that is unless an English boy falls off the terraces in Macchpicchu!

Wednesday and off to another airport. Checking in was slow and erratic with a lot of queue jumping Whilst waiting for the plane I got into conversation with a young lady who had been staying at the same hotel as I had in Cusco. The young lady was travelling around South America in the opposite direction to me. We talked about the churches we had seen and she said that, if I had had enough of churches, I should visit a museum in Lima which had a large collection of erotic pottery. I decided to bear this in mind.

On arriving in Lima I returned to the Hotel Crillon. After booking in I called on two lawyers in a law firm on my list. One of them had just returned from his honeymoon in London and other parts of Europe. Both lawyers had been to Harvard. Here I might point out that many of the lawyers I saw had some American or British connection. The two men took me to their club for an excellent lunch (prawns and sea bass). I then went on to call on yet another manager of the Bank of London & South America. After this appointment I went to look at the main square which was as in Cusco called the Plaza de Armas. I took some photographs of the Cathedral and the Government Palace whilst fending off the shoeshine boys who were most persistent. On one of the pavements next to the magazines and paintings which were everywhere there were sitting at tables over a dozen chess players concentrating on their games. I think it was a case of turn up and play whoever was waiting. On my way back to the hotel I caught my foot in one of the many holes in the pavements, but fortunately did no real damage. I had no wish to explore the inside of a Peruvian hospital. I ended the day with dinner in the hotel Sky Room which had a marvellous panoramic view of the city and also allowed me to watch the floor show whilst I ate. The Peruvian dancers who performed that evening did a number of marineras which is a courtship dance where both dancers use large handkerchiefs as props. It was quite charming.

On Thursday I woke with a sore throat. Ugh! My first appointment was with a firm of lawyers with offices on the fifteenth floor of a modern office block. The partner I saw told me that his firm had been founder members of a South American law club, but that problems had arisen because two of the partners in one of the member firms were wanted by the police, having been accused of a gigantic tax fraud. As I understand it the two men, who were partners in a Mexican law firm of very high standing, were accused of setting up a bogus company to which a large number of corporations paid money for goods and services that were never supplied. After a deduction of ten per cent the money was later returned and presumably did not find its way into the various companies' books. It was reported that the two men had fled the country in January 1980 with $18 million. Just one of the problems of running a law club I thought.

On my way to the next appointment I did not feel too well so I went into a rather rough café-bar and had a local brandy. Amazingly I soon felt better. The next lawyer I saw was a very friendly man with, I hope he will forgive me for saying so, a considerable girth. On my return to the hotel I saw in the street a row of stands with typewriters on them. Next to them stood a series of clerks, all male, who would take instructions from anybody who wanted a letter written or a document prepared.

Back at the hotel I tried to ring home, but there was a three hour delay so I gave up and went for a walk to the Plaza de Armas where I visited the Cathedral. Apparently Francisco Pizarro, the conqueror of the Incas, laid the foundation stone on 18 January 1535, the day on which the city of Lima was itself founded. One of the exhibits I saw was a casket reputedly containing Pizarro's remains - an appropriate resting place. The Church of San Pedro was shut so I went to see the Torre Tagle Palace, a building with beautiful wooden carved balconies. Next I saw La Merced, a church with a very elaborate front and another golden interior. I then walked back to the hotel past the ever present shoeshine boys, racks of magazines and paintings which were of high quality and in certain areas glass cases containing exotic butterflies and spiders. I would have liked to buy a case of the exotic butterflies, but I did not think it would have fitted into my suitcase. In the evening I had another local brandy and began to feel much better.

On Friday I was booked on to a very early flight to Quito, the capital of Ecuador. However when I arrived at Lima airport I found that my flight had been cancelled. No explanation was given. There were no other flights to Quito that day, so I booked a flight for the following day but with no great confidence. The airline did though give me a voucher to cover my expenses, but this did not make up for losing a day in Ecuador and missing out on the appointments I had made. I accordingly went back to my hotel and after lunch decided to follow the advice given to me earlier by my fellow traveller.

The Larco Museum is said to house over 50,000 items of pre-Columbian art, but is particularly well known for its room of erotic pottery. I looked around various rooms and then came to the room of erotica. As I looked at the pottery and tried to understand the exhibit cards which were written in Spanish I was aware that I was being watched quite closely by an armed policewoman, the only other occupant of the room; I would guess that this attractive lady was about 20 years old. Seeing that I was having difficulty translating the Spanish and no doubt wishing to try out her English, the policewoman came across and offered to help. I readily agreed. At this point I was looking at pottery that somewhat resembled Toby jugs. They were drinking vessels with expressive handles. "This" the policewoman said "is a man making love to a woman." "And this is a man making love to a man", she continued. "And this" she said "is a woman making love to a dog." This was too much for me and I went bright red. The young policewoman was however completely unfazed and went on to describe even more strange couplings. I must say that the tourist police had a real find in this young policewoman as she was very dutiful, spending an hour or so showing me round. During this somewhat bizarre experience I did wonder what my partners would think if they could have seen me at that point. It was altogether an unforgettable experience. Back at my hotel I again dined in the restaurant with the floorshow. I am really getting my fill of Peruvian music and dance.

My plane did not leave Lima until 12.30 p.m. on Saturday so I had a short stroll around the city in the morning. My initial impression of Lima was that it was scruffy and I had not changed that view, but it did have some very fine buildings. I thought I had plenty of time, but the hotel bus never turned up and I took another bus which did not arrive at the airport until 12 noon. This meant that I had to jump the queue. Ironically the plane then left late.

The hotel I stayed at in Quito was in a beautiful situation with land sloping steeply away from the gardens and into the jungle. In the bar of the hotel I got into conversation with an interesting man, a representative of a steel corporation in Cleveland, Ohio. He told me that he had the ability to blot out pain by will power. I thought about testing this by giving the man a really hard kick, but on reflection felt that he might misunderstand my motives and I restrained myself. Because I arrived a day late I had no business appointments, but although I could see the lights of the city from the hotel I did not have the energy to explore it. The sun set at 6 p.m. It always does because we were only 15 miles from the equator. Likewise the sun always rises at 6 a.m. For once early to bed.

On Sunday I took an early taxi and asked the driver to take the tourist route to the airport. Quito is a fine city, redolent of its Spanish past and in comparison with Lima seemed to me clean and less scruffy. The buildings have ornate balconies and one can easily imagine a Spanish troubadour serenading his loved one from below. In one street we went through there was a market going on and people shopping crossed regularly in front of the taxi without ever looking - fortunately we hit nobody, not even the woman who was breastfeeding at the same time. This time I was at the airport early. The plane stopped at Guayaquil for half an hour or so, but eventually I arrived in Caracas, the capital of Venezuela. It took ages to get through the airport, and it was about 8 p.m. when I arrived at the Inter-Continental, a very nice hotel. I really had been travelling all day. The weather was fine so I was able to sit in an outside restaurant and dine whilst I listened to the music and watched the dancing. It was close to midnight when I got to bed somewhat tired.

143

On Monday I started my day by calling on a law firm who had also been members of the same South American law club as the law firm in Lima that I had visited. I was told that they broke away about a year before and therefore they avoided any link with the scandal. I then called on another law firm and saw a charming man who seemed to me to be to be very efficient. The lawyer told me that he planned each day and kept computer records of time spent. Although now almost universal in England, this was not so in 1980. He also told me that communications with Europe took between three and eight weeks - no emails then. We had an excellent lunch together (back to steaks thank heavens) and I then went on to the British Embassy and after seeing a representative there I went on to Lloyds Bank International. The manager of the bank told me that he had been to Whitgift School in Croydon and knew one of our articled clerks who was a fellow student. He also knew the bank manager I had met at Machupicchu. It's a small world!

After dinner at the hotel I bumped into the steel man I had met in Ecuador who was with his Venezuelan associate. We had some drinks and the Venezuelan told me that Venezuela had the highest per capita income in South America. I said that, in view of the horrendous traffic jams I had experienced, the citizens of Caracas must all own cars. "Well," he said "you are not that far out because the authorities, concerned at the traffic congestion in Caracas, prohibited certain vehicles entering the city on particular days." "This was accomplished" he said "by categorising the vehicles according to the first letter on their number plate and then forbidding vehicles in a certain category to enter the city on two days each week." As I understood this plan a vehicle with a number plate having any starting letter from e.g. A to K would not be allowed in the city on e.g. Mondays and Thursdays. "Did it work?" I asked. "No" said the Venezuelan because all the rich people just bought extra cars with different number plates. The authorities should, I thought, have anticipated that possibility.

On Tuesday I was on my way to Panama City, but Caracas airport was in complete chaos. The representative at the check in desk told me I needed gate 30, but the board showed gate 23 so I went to gate 23 only to be told by the man at the gate that I needed gate 22. The man at immigration however said I should go to gate 24 and I was on my way there when the loudspeaker announced that the gate for the flight to Panama City was 13. I altered my route, but when I had nearly reached the gate I heard a correction. "Please go to gate 14." When I got there I found that it was gate 13 after all. This sort of thing is not an unusual occurrence when travelling around South America, but it makes what is fascinating sometimes frustrating too.

After checking in to the Continental Hotel I called on a banker and then I went on to the British Embassy where to my surprise I was seen by our Ambassador. After lunch I visited another law firm and then back to the hotel for a rest. Part of the hotel lobby was a sort of casino. I am not a gambler, but I did try the slot machines because if you won bells rang and there was a lovely tinkling sound as tens to hundreds of coins of very small value came tumbling out. In the evening after dinner I got into conversation in the bar with an English shipping representative and he introduced me to planters punch, a very nice drink in that sort of climate. Whilst drinking we listened to a Wurlitzer Organ which originally came from Atlantic City. The various parts were coloured in fluorescent paint and moved as the organ was played - truly hypnotic. I later discovered that the organ had 2,200 pipes, 4,000 electric magnets and 8,000 small bellows. It was quite a beast.

On Wednesday I had an 8.30 a.m. appointment with a law firm which had very modern offices and then to a law firm with four partners, all being members of the same family. The father told me that he had studied law at University College and had a flat in London. One of the sons asked me to join him for lunch at his home, but said I must bring a swimming costume, so I returned to the hotel and was picked up later. The villa, which I assumed belonged to the father, was absolutely beautiful. There was a largish swimming pool which had a waterfall and the garden contained an abundance of tropical trees and plants. I enjoyed my swim and the excellent lunch of lobster, rice and salad which we ate by the pool. "This is the life" I thought. My reflections were interrupted by the son who said "I really envy you as you have seasons when things change, whereas here it is nearly always the same." I must admit I had never thought of it that way. The son knew what he was talking about because he had lived in Cambridge for some time.

Back at the hotel I thought that I cannot visit Panama without seeing the canal. This thought was reinforced by my guide to Panama which said that visiting Panama without taking a look at the canal was like visiting Raquel Welch without taking a look below the eyebrows! Accordingly I took a taxi to the Miraflores Locks. Unfortunately I was too late in the day to see any vessels going through, but the canal itself was very impressive. After dinner out (I was particularly taken with ceviche - delicious citrus marinated raw fish) I spent another evening drinking planters punches and listening to and watching the amazing organ. I am now nearing the end of my trip as tomorrow is my last country: Mexico.

On Thursday I checked in at Panama City airport for my flight to Mexico City. As I did not have anything to read on the flight I looked in a magazine kiosk, but the only thing I could find written in English was a Playboy magazine (truly!).

146

After a three hour flight I stood in a long queue. When I got to the head of the queue an officious customs officer decided to go through my belongings with some care. He even squeezed the toothpaste out of its tube and smelled it, presumably looking for some prohibited drug. Then he came to the Playboy magazine. To my embarrassment he opened it up and holding the centrefold out for all to see tut tutted. There were still quite a large number of people behind me in the queue and to my further discomfort some of them joined in the tut tutting. I expected that the customs officer would confiscate my magazine on the grounds that it might corrupt the morals of the Mexican people but he handed it back to me, rather like a headmaster returning one's catapult with the implication that it would be better destroyed.

For some reason I was not feeling too well, so after checking into my hotel I had a sandwich and decided to go to bed early. After about an hour a lady knocked on my door and I answered it dressed in a bathrobe; she asked me if Senor Thompson was about and I said that he must have booked out. The lady then looked over my shoulder to check that I was on my own and said "Would you like me to join you?" I said "No thank you I am very tired tonight" The "lady" then left and I realised that I might quite inadvertently have suggested that I might be available the following night. In any event I never saw her again. I must have led a sheltered life because this was the only occasion in my life that I have been accosted in a hotel.

Friday and back to work. First a lawyer whose firm had a staff of two hundred and then a partner in another large firm who told me that they had too much work and were having difficulty in obtaining bright young lawyers - who usually came via London or the U.S.A. I then called on the British Consul and a bank manager. Most of my lunch break though was spent at the Pan Am offices as British Airways were on strike and I had to rearrange my flight home by another route. After about an hour or so I managed to book a ticket to Heathrow, so I carried on with my appointments, another law firm and the chamber of commerce.

Mexico City was bustling, but although there was clearly a lot of wealth around dire poverty (or what I assumed to be dire poverty) was ever present. The pavements were full of beggars, many of whom were missing a limb or two. It is of course possible that these beggars were very successful and had lots of money. I just do not know. Back at the hotel I decided to go on an organised night tour. Apart from me there were a couple from Alaska, a young lady from Kansas and two young ladies from Los Angeles. No trouble with the language this time! We had dinner in a restaurant in a park and then went to Garibaldi Square. This is where the Mariachis, Mexicans in sombreros wearing trousers with black and white stripes on them, serenade anybody who asks (and pays). On to a night club that had Mexican dancers, cowboys with spinning ropes and an extraordinary slow motion acrobatic troupe. Finally on to another club which had a very good flamenco show. Inevitably I was late to bed.

On Saturday I went on a cultural/historical tour with two men and a couple, all from the U.S.A. Our first stop was the Basilica of Our Lady of Guadalupe, apparently the second most visited Catholic shrine in the world. It has several million visitors a year. In December 2009, for example, over six million people visited the Basilica over a two day period. The church accommodates some fifty thousand people who can attend mass at any time of the day - as it is continuous (or was when I was there). The new Basilica had only just been finished some four years before my visit and it is an interesting modern building that to me looked more like a football stadium. The Image of Our Lady can be seen by an escalator-moving crowd. The tradition is that in 1531 a poor

Indian saw a vision of a lady who told him to build a church on the spot where they were standing. The peasant reported this to the local bishop who asked for proof that this was indeed the Virgin Mary. The Indian returned to the same place and the vision reappeared and left its image on his humble cloak - and that is what you see if you believe in the tradition.

The tour then went on to Teotihuacan, the City of the Gods. This is where you can see the Pyramids of the Sun and the Moon, comparable in size to the Great Pyramids of Egypt. They are very impressive structures, but not the only ones. There are many other stepped structures in a site which originally covered over 11 square miles. It must have been a large and imposing city at its peak. Tourists were climbing up and down the numerous steps that centuries ago had been cut into the sides of the pyramids and I joined in, but half way up my pyramid I had an attack of vertigo and had to climb down in a sitting position. This was particularly humiliating as nobody else seemed affected. Indeed a little Indian boy was running up and down selling tourist items, one of which I bought. There was a large open space in the middle of the site, the size of many football pitches, and as I walked across it I had a very strong feeling of what it must have been like when human sacrifices took place there (I assume this did in fact happen). The whole area had for me amazing atmosphere. A truly splendid place to visit.

Back in Mexico City I walked to San Francisco Church - another elaborate gilded altar - and then to the Cathedral with two gilded altars. Finally I went to the President's Palace, an imposing building with a frontage of over 650 feet. There is a lot to see in Mexico City, but by now I was getting a little jaded by churches and palaces so I called it a day. On return to my hotel I rested and watched some television. A programme broadcast in the U.S.A. was on and I was somewhat amused when the lady giving the weather forecast said that the following day the weather in her area would be "peachy perfect." Not what you would get from the BBC I thought. I finished the final day of my trip with a typical Mexican meal including my last ceviche followed by my last tequila.

On Sunday I was booked to fly home on a Pan Am flight, which was scheduled to go to Heathrow via Houston and New York. At Houston, although in transit, I still had to go through immigration. The immigration officer asked me for my American visa and I explained that I did not have one as I had never intended to return to England via the U.S.A. and would not have done so if British Airways had not gone on strike. The officer explained that, as I was landing at two American cities, I was an immigrant and, as I had no visa, therefore an illegal immigrant. I was technically arrested and my ticket and passport were confiscated and given to an air stewardess. I was told not to leave the airport, but report back when the plane was ready for boarding. In the end all was well, but I did wonder if my name went into the computer records as an undesirable person.

The officials at New York were much more relaxed and I had a memorable flight back to Heathrow. I was the only passenger in first class which was in the upper level of the plane. Because of this I had a stewardess all to myself. She cooked me lemon sole and apologised in case it was not all right because, as she explained, it was her maiden flight in the first class section and she was accordingly somewhat inexperienced.. In fact the lemon sole was very good indeed. Heathrow when I landed was covered by a bank of grey cloud. After sunny South America this was a rude awakening. Some welcome back to England I thought.

In one calendar month I had visited eight countries and travelled over 20,000 miles. Perhaps not an unusual itinerary for a businessman promoting his company's products but less usual for a lawyer, I suspect. In the course of my trip I had met a number of very interesting people and I had seen some marvellous sights. I also learned what it is like to live on one's own for such a length of time - personally I prefer to have somebody with me to talk over the day's events. Nevertheless it was a fascinating experience which I am very glad I had.

I apologise to the reader for referring to my business appointments which may be of little interest to him or her but if I had left them out I would have given the impression that I was on a jolly whereas I did in fact work very hard when I had "my business suit on." My records show that I made contact with 67 different individuals and the real number would have been a lot higher. To keep on "giving a performance" for a whole month was quite a test of my resilience.

CHAPTER EIGHT

The Quality Law Group

In or about 1992 Russell Bell, who was one of my Croydon partners, had the idea of forming a British law club involving initially 10 law firms from England and two from Scotland. I had nothing to do with the formation of the club, but I very shortly became heavily involved with one aspect of setting it up. At the inaugural meeting in Bristol discussion took place as to how the club could distinguish itself from other similar clubs. It was suggested that the key element should be the quality of its service. This was agreed as was the proposed name "The Quality Law Group." I personally thought this was a hostage to fortune because clients, I believed, would thereafter be critical of even the smallest failing. The next issue was how could the club achieve a consistently high level of service across 12 law firms with different cultures and in two cases with different laws and procedures. The answer we came up with was that each firm should seek and acquire accreditation under B.S.5750 (now ISO 9001). This was a substantial task for everybody, but particularly for those like me who were appointed Quality Controllers for their firms. I remember telling the other attendants at the first meeting that when I started in the law I had wanted to become a barrister and that, although I had taken a different path, I had now achieved my earlier ambition and become a Q.C.

Before moving on I should explain what B.S.5750 was. B.S. stood for British Standard and 5750 had the following requirements for any firm that wished to be certified: a set of procedures that covered all key processes; monitoring of processes to ensure they were effective; keeping adequate records; checking for defects and taking corrective action; regularly reviewing individuals and the quality system itself; and facilitating continual improvement. It should be noted that the system did not ensure that the right advice was given or the right action taken. It was like grading a restaurant by checking all their systems for buying and storing food, the cleanliness of the kitchen, the speed and helpfulness of the waiters or waitresses, but ignoring the quality of the cooking. The reason for this is that it is very difficult to grade legal advice or action unless it is palpably wrong. For example, if six experienced probate lawyers drafted a complex will, it would probably be difficult to grade their draft wills in order of excellence, even perhaps with detailed consideration by an expert draftsman - and this would be wholly impracticable in any event.

The first task I had was to look at and write up the existing procedures in our three offices. Unsurprisingly I found that few procedures were already written down and that there were marked differences between the ways in which each office operated. I then had to look at all the procedures to see if they complied with the British Standard as where they did not the procedure had to be suitably altered and the new procedure put in writing.

Before I began though I started to think about what the word "quality" meant. It was not I considered a synonym for excellence and in reference to the British Standard did not relate, as already explained, to the quality of the legal advice or action taken. My definition was that quality in this context was meeting or exceeding the client's perception of what their solicitor would do for them. Before seeing a solicitor a client will have formed some perception, however vague it may be, of what the solicitor will do, how long it will take and how much it will cost. The client may be out, possibly widely so, in one, two or three respects. Take the example of buying a small farmhouse with some land. The client may think that it is a straightforward matter, that it will take no longer than a couple of months and that it will not cost more than one thousand pounds. In a particular case the client might be found to be optimistic on every count. There could be boundary disputes, problems over rights of way and so on which could be difficult to resolve and which would increase both the time and the cost. In such circumstances a wise solicitor would correct these wrong assumptions at the beginning and explain to the client the likely pitfalls and the delays that might lie ahead. If this is not done then however good a job the solicitor actually does the client will not think he has had good service. The solicitor's perception of his own performance is frankly irrelevant. If however the client's perceptions are not only met, but exceeded then he will think he has got a bargain.

What "quality" is also varies from client to client. For example a client buying a house might require his solicitor to bother him as little as possible and keep the fees to a minimum. If however the solicitor then sends fortnightly reports on progress and copies all incoming letters to the client because that is what he normally does he is not listening to the client and the client will not be pleased - irrespective of how good a job the solicitor has actually done. All of what I have said may seem fairly obvious now, but at the time I am writing about I suspect this was less so.

The Law Society had already pushed solicitors in the right direction by making it a rule that a letter be sent to the client at the outset setting out certain matters. In particular the solicitor was to remind the client what instructions he had given, what advice the solicitor had put forward, what action the solicitor was going to take, what were the likely costs, what billing arrangements had been agreed and to whom the client could address any complaints.. This letter could now be expanded to also inform clients about any possible difficulties that might be encountered as their case progressed.

Among the papers I kept on my retirement was one I wrote in October 1991 on "Quality Control" so it appears that this subject was on my mind before the formation of The Quality Law Group. It was a paper written primarily for the London office partners and staff. In it I put forward three slogans which were "a good quality service at a fair fee", "first impressions count" and "the client is (nearly) always right." I pointed out that we had to improve the quality of our service by starting with people and attitudes and that the first problem was to get everybody in the firm to think in the same way about quality issues. I stated that we were all individuals and that some were tidy and some untidy, some were punctual and some unpunctual, but nevertheless each job should be carried out to the standard that that job required.

I suggested that individual weaknesses could sometimes be hidden. For example if a lawyer's room was very untidy (not an unusual occurrence) clients should always be seen in designated interview rooms. I added that the effect could then be spoiled if the file was falling to pieces. At the end of the paper I set out a series of questions and asked each fee earner to mark themselves out of 10 on each question. By way of example: "Are the letters to the client clear and to the point, correct in grammar and spelling and neatly typed? Have you answered incoming letters within two to three days of receipt? Have you returned telephone calls the same day? Have you kept a client who comes to the office on an appointment waiting longer than five minutes? Do you go through all your files once a month?" The results of this test were sometimes illuminating, although I did wonder how honest my colleagues had been in marking themselves. One thing however was clear and that was that different standards were being applied in different parts of the London office. I was in the course of addressing this difference in attitude when events overtook me. The need to get B.S.5750 would I felt solve my problem as the quality standard would be imposed from outside rather than by me as one partner seemingly imposing my will on others. What I did not then know is what troubles I was bringing on myself.

I suppose I had the right cast of mind for the job of Quality Controller. I have always been very tidy and I was a great believer in managing one's time to get the most out of the working day. I can exemplify this by describing a typical day. I should though point out that this was before emails had become a popular method of communication.

I would start at about 9.15 a.m. and sit down at an empty desk (all the files were put away overnight). I would then look at my diary to see what lay ahead. The post would be brought in and I would read each letter and put it in one of three piles: the first of the piles was for filing or simple acknowledgment, which my secretary could deal with, the second was for a reply to be dictated there and then and the third was for further consideration and formation of a reply. I believe Perry Mason had a similar practice. As my filing cabinets were in my office I would get out the files I wanted and start dictating on tape the replies to the more straightforward letters. I would try and get the tape to my secretary as soon as possible so that she could start typing the replies and then I would start on a second tape and so on until I had finished all but the more complicated letters. Curiously I found that if I had read the "tough letters" through in the morning my subconscious went to work and I could deal with them much more easily in the afternoon. During this morning session I was unavailable to anybody unless there was an emergency. Telephone callers were told that I would ring them back.

When I had finished morning dictation my secretary would give me my telephone messages and I would ring back each caller in turn. I would then spend the next session in legal research, preparing documents, dictating instructions to

156

barristers to appear in court and such like. Again I was incommunicado. At the end of this period I would check again as to telephone messages and I would ring back each caller and also make any calls that I wished to make. Generally I would take lunch at about 1 p.m. The afternoon was for appointments and I would have my first appointment at 2 p.m. and possibly another one at 4 p.m. When the second caller had left I would read the letters I had dictated, correct any errors and sign off the final version. I would then check again on telephone messages and ring back each caller. The end of the working day was for discussions with partners and colleagues and "tidying up." Of course the day I have described is one where I had no court appointments and in reality the structured pattern was usually interrupted a number of times by something or other - but having such a pattern worked for me.

Writing the office manual was the first task to achieve B.S.5750 accreditation and a formidable one it was too. We engaged a consultant who worked from a precedent. Something as a lawyer I should understand. However the consultant did not like straying from his precedent which was extremely turgid, complex and long. He wanted 20 quality procedures with an underlying layer of work instructions. I cut this down to ten quality procedures and no work instructions. It was still though full of detail. I shall give some examples. If a file was taken out of its filing cabinet a large card had to be put in its place indicating who had taken the file and when. This caused real irritation when only one fee earner was working on the file. Every file had to have a case plan in the front setting out the client's objectives and how they were to be achieved and this had to be updated every time a fee earner took some action on the file. This was again an irritation, particularly to conveyancers who often worked on their files without help and used to tell me that they knew what they were doing and did not need a case plan to remind them.

157

Books in the library that were out of date had to have stickers attached on the front cover setting out a warning to this effect. One of my Croydon partners, who had a wry sense of humour, had his wedding photograph on his desk and as he had been married many years he attached such a sticker stating: "warning this photo (book had been crossed out) is out of date." Sometimes it was difficult to get my colleagues to take things seriously!

Telephone calls had to be answered before the third ring and if the fee earner was unavailable and a response was required had to be returned the same or the following day by the fee earner or if still unavailable by an apologetic secretary. An approved list of barristers and experts had to be kept and feedback added if somebody on the list was instructed. Experts had to present their c.v.'s and these had to be checked. If anybody breached a quality procedure or was aware of one being breached a non- conformance report had to be filled in. It is not difficult to imagine how unpopular this was. I have so far only given a small sample of the manual's requirements, but I hope I have conveyed its flavour. It took a lot of hard work, but eventually the manual was finished. My secretary at the time did a fantastic job and I would not have managed this task without her considerable help.

The next step in the process was distributing copies of the manual to everybody in the firm and training all the partners and staff on putting the procedures into effect. This understandably took some considerable time, but eventually all were trained and we had a dry run before seeking accreditation. One of the quality procedures was to check that all the other procedures were being followed. This entailed spot checks by a small group of partners in each office. Each one of them was also subject to the same scrutiny by another member of the group. I as the Quality Controller then kept a file with the reports in and I had to interview miscreants and ascertain how they intended to correct their "non-conformances" in the future. This whole procedure was very time consuming and very unpopular. However despite murmurings of possible dissent progress was being made and I decided that it was time for the inspectors to call.

If my memory is correct the inspectors were with us at the London office for a couple of days during which I had to be available at all times to answer any queries that they might have. It was a fairly traumatic experience. The inspectors checked everything with great care. At the end of the inspection the two inspectors met up with me and said that the London office would have passed, but for one thing. Apparently the inspectors had carried out a spot check on one of my partners who was a conveyancer and they had asked him why he had signed a particular form at the front of the file. I should here explain that under the procedures every file contained such a form. It set out the client's instructions very briefly and the fee earner's signature thereunder signified that he or she had understood those instructions and was confirming that they had the legal skills to deal with the matter, the available time to do the job properly and that there was no conflict with the work of any other client of the firm. I knew from a preliminary visit that this was a matter that the inspectors considered particularly important and I had briefed my partners and other fee earners to make sure they gave the right reply. "What did he say?" I asked the inspectors. "He said" they responded "that he had signed the form because Stuart Duncan told him to do so." I could have wept. After all the hard work I had put in it meant a delay of some months, further disruption of my own legal work followed by another long inspection.

Fortunately next time the inspectors passed all the offices and we got our accreditation. I had by now learnt my lesson and had picked dates for the London office inspection when my errant partner was on holiday. Despite the delay I believe that we were still one of the first firms in London to obtain B.S. 5750 accreditation. The other firms in the Group also obtained accreditation and the Group began to function. I attended meetings in Edinburgh, Birmingham and elsewhere, but when the London office of my firm merged with Bircham & Co we had to leave the Group as Bircham & Co did not have B.S. 5750 accreditation. Bircham & Co did consider going down the same path, but I was in some ways relieved that they did not as I suspect that I would then have spent the last couple of years or so of my career as a solicitor in reprising my role as a Q.C.

My views on B.S. 5750 were and are ambivalent. I agreed with many of the procedures, but maintaining the Standard required a great deal of form filling and took up a great deal of time. I and to a lesser extent others had therefore less time to devote to our clients' affairs. This was not I thought good professionally or economically.

As guidelines for good practice the manual I helped produce had, I believe, real merit, but that of course was not how it was in fact used. The real difficulty I appreciate is that if the procedures in the manual are not mandatory then they are much less likely to be followed. I realise of course that standards and targets are very much in vogue these days, but I note with interest the negative reactions to them from the police, teachers etc. I myself believe that whatever procedures are adopted the procedures and their implementation should take away the least time possible from doing the core job.

CHAPTER NINE

Allied Activities

In this part of my reminiscences I shall be looking back on activities that were in one way or another connected to my job but were not actually part of it in the strictest sense of the word. There will be as throughout this work a number of diversions.

Commuting I do not look back on with any great fondness, although there must statistically have been some enjoyable moments. Over the years my journey length varied from half an hour each way to just over two hours each way at the end of my career. I can hardly now believe that I coped with over four hours commuting a day but I did, although I was by then working part time. Travelling can on occasions be dangerous, but I suppose the closest shave that I ever had was on 18 November 1987 when we had a late partners meeting and afterwards a number of us went to the Naval and Military club which was nearby for a drink. At about 7 p.m. I said that I was going home, but I was prevailed upon to have another drink. If I had not succumbed, I would have been in the Kings Cross station complex just when the serious fire broke out that killed over 30 people. Of course if I had left earlier I could have been run over crossing the road on the way to the underground station, but somehow just missing being involved in a major disaster seemed a matter of significance.

For many years I commuted by train from Radlett in Hertfordshire. I often travelled with the same group of fellow passengers and, although we had interesting conversations, I usually did "The Times" crossword at the same time. Three of my travelling companions were each called David and by chance two of them were also solicitors. One morning one of the Davids said to me "Why don't you and David have a race to see who can finish the crossword first." I agreed and as I thought about the answers I was aware of my opponent filling in the blank squares with regular strokes of his pen. We were about eight or so minutes into our journey, when David said "I've finished it." I was at that point less than half way through my crossword. I was extremely impressed with David's speed, but as I congratulated him the others started to laugh. I had been tricked. When David had arrived at the station he had already finished his crossword whilst having a leisurely breakfast. One of the other Davids however suggested playing a joke on me and he exchanged his clean copy of "The Times" with David's marked one. I was completely taken in. The three Davids, however, had smiles on their faces for the whole journey.

Another commuting incident that amused me at the time involved a West Indian railwayman who used to come on to the station at Radlett to make announcements using a tannoy system. One morning he strode out and said "Da next train will stop at Kings Cross only" in a pronounced West Indian accent. Normally trains stopped at Elstree and occasionally at West Hampstead, so a straight through train was a bonus. The train then approached the station and the expectant passengers all took a step forward, but to our surprise the train did not stop at all. The announcement was literally correct as "the "next train" was indeed scheduled to stop at Kings Cross only.

The other commuting memory I have when I was living at Radlett is cycling to and from work once a week for about six or seven weeks if my memory is correct. It was in 1989 and the railway union had called an all out strike on each Wednesday of every week until eventually the dispute was resolved. I was determined not to be beaten by the strike and, although I was in my fifties, I was reasonably fit and I therefore decided to pedal in to London and back on my trusty bike. Going in by car would have been horrendous because of the amount of cars on the road and the difficulty of parking when I got to Mayfair. Overall I was lucky with the weather and I rather enjoyed it. I particularly liked cycling through Regent's Park and overtaking one stationary car after another on the inside. This was though a slightly hazardous manoeuvre as in those days most people smoked and the front seat passengers were wont to lean out of their window and casually throw out cigarette stubs without consideration for any passing cyclists, but I was lucky and never got knocked off my bike. I often wondered if what I did was doing me good or harm. The exercise was no doubt beneficial, but the exhaust fumes that I breathed in were certainly not. The length of my journey was almost exactly 20 miles each way and my record for one leg was getting home one day in 90 minutes. As there were two proper hills on the way, namely Hampstead and Mill Hill, I do not think this was too bad a time. In the event I did not miss a single working day so I think I did beat the strike after all.

For some years I used to commute on the tube from Hampstead to central London. I recall an incident one evening on my way home. I noticed that a man who was standing was pestering a young woman who was sitting down. The young woman was trying to ignore him, but the man continued to bother her. I asked the man to leave her alone but he then became quite aggressive. Fortunately we were just approaching Hampstead station and, as the young woman lived in Hampstead too, we both got up to get off the train. The man however followed and I hastened my travelling companion down the tunnel towards the lift. The doors were about to close so I pushed the young lady in and jumped in myself. We eluded the aggressive traveller, but I got caught in the lift doors. The lift was full and as the shaft was very deep it took some time to get to the surface. I was wearing a raincoat at the time and, as the lift doors snagged it, I was held tight whilst the buttons on my raincoat shot off like bullets. I tried to look nonchalant, but I don't think I succeeded. Looking nonchalant when spread eagled inside a lift which seemed to take ages to get to the surface was by no means an easy task.

As already mentioned I regularly did "The Times" crossword when commuting. Later when su doku became popular I became addicted to the killer version. During tube journeys though it was often difficult to open one's paper to the right page in the crush (Why oh why did "The Times" take its cryptic crossword off the back page - fortunately now after a long gap restored to its rightful place). On the occasions when a crowded tube prevented me opening my newspaper I sometimes thought up poems in my head which I later refined and wrote down. One effort was my attempt to write a verse using numbers in their correct order hidden in each line of verse.

The little poem called "URA1" went as follows:

"Indeed you are a 1
2 know is such delight;
Wi3lly quite a knack
4 making me feel bright.
If 5 got naught to do
And feel in a 6tate,
It7 to think of you
And long I'll medit8.
I think of you your eyes be9
And of your 10derness;
Then naught do I desire,
But you in my caress."

I have often found it satisfying to put my thoughts into poetry and throughout my adult life I have regularly used the verse form in speeches and toasts - indeed on one occasion I recall giving the chairman's annual report at a P.T.A. meeting in verse to the surprise of all those present, including my wife who had not been forewarned.

My number poem is also a sort of example of my love of puns, in common with Shakespeare I might add. My favourite pun was made many years ago. I and three other husbands used to get together to cook a special evening meal for our wives once each year. One year it just so happened that we picked D Day for our dinner date and we decided to have a second world war theme for our menu. I was in charge of the main course and, although we had a veal dish the year before, I decided to do veal ragout. This I described on the menu as "Veal Meat Again" (if you don't get the pun look up Vera Lynn on the internet). Double puns are hard enough to think up, but triple puns are truly rare. Indeed the only example I can recall is the story of the three young men who emigrated to America and bought a cattle ranch. The boys however could not agree what to call the ranch so they sent a cable to their father in England asking for his advice. In due course the father cabled back: "Call the ranch Focus." The three ranchers were baffled, so they cabled their father again asking him: "Why Focus?" After a short delay a further cable arrived. It read: "Because that's where the sons raise meat."

I have always felt that my firm, whatever its stage of development, was a friendly place in which to work. We always had excellent parties at Christmas or when somebody hit a special birthday or retired and our office outings, especially during the Stoneham Langton & Passmore period, were greatly enjoyed by everyone. It was for the partners in particular a good occasion to get to know better the members of the firm who worked in the other offices, including their other partners. One of the favourite outings was a river trip on the Thames. This suited everybody. There was food and drink on board, music for dancing to and interesting riverside properties to look at.

We would usually board the boat which was reserved for the firm at Charing Cross and then go up river to somewhere like Kew or down river to somewhere like Greenwich. On one trip we boarded at Kingston, I think, and ended up at Windsor. It was a firm tradition to stop somewhere in the afternoon and play a game of rounders. The match was usually the men against the women and I am sorry to say that the women, whose number was greater, cheated dreadfully and often therefore won. I recall on one occasion we stopped at an unoccupied island in the Thames to play our rounders match. We had our usual heavily contested game and it was only when we had travelled a number of miles down the river that we realised that we had left one of our number (the office receptionist) stranded on the island. I later discovered that our colleague had to wave down a passing boat and persuade the captain to give him a lift. In any event our marooned colleague was at his post on the Monday morning, albeit in a somewhat grumpy mood - unfortunately for us a not completely unheard of situation.

On one occasion we took the whole of the firm to France on a day trip. As our coach arrived at the Channel early in the morning I was telling one of our senior lawyers, a man in his late fifties or early sixties, a story about my mother in law who on the night before my wife and I were taking her to France on holiday calmly announced that she did not have a passport. Instead of smiling at my anecdote my colleague said that he did not have a passport either. "But" I said "you once told me that you had been to Egypt and various other countries in North Africa." My colleague then explained that all his foreign journeys were made during the war when he did not need a passport to invade Africa and that he had never actually travelled abroad since. Somehow we smuggled our senior lawyer into France without a passport and without any of us getting arrested.

On arrival in France our coach took us to a very attractive open air restaurant just south of Le Touquet and after a splendid lunch two of the younger lawyers put on a mock Oscars ceremony. I think, if I remember correctly, I got the Oscar for best supporting male role for my realistic portrayal of the slave driver in "Ben Hur". We then stopped at Le Touquet to buy cheeses and suchlike. On our return crossing of the Channel, although I was at the time still something of a beginner, I made up a bridge four with the senior partner, Grant Middleton, and two absolute beginners. The bridge was I am sorry to say of a very low standard, but despite our overall lack of ability it was an enjoyable end to an enjoyable day. I say "end" because just about everybody slept soundly during the coach ride back to London.

Talking of bridge reminds me of going to bridge classes in Chelsea. At the first lesson our teacher was late and a rather bossy lady, who was some kind of civil servant, suggested that some of us played a few hands whilst we waited. The bossy lady asked me to play and I agreed because I had played before. The lady's eyes then lit upon a young couple who explained that they had never played bridge before. The bossy lady insisted and the young couple sat down and the cards were dealt. The bossy lady made no bid and it was the young lady's turn to bid next. "What do I do?" she asked. "Give yourself four points for an ace, three for a king, two for a queen and one for a jack, add them up and if you have thirteen points or more bid one of your longest suit" the bossy lady replied. I could see that the young lady was trembling with anxiety. She thought for some time and I could almost hear her counting her points. She was going to bid. A small and uncertain voice then said "What are the ones that look like blackberries called?" This somewhat amazing question stopped the bossy lady in her tracks. It had never occurred to her that somebody would come to bridge classes, never having played cards before. Sadly the young couple never returned after their first lesson - it was clearly all too much for them.

And then there were our cricket matches. It all started at the time Raymond Pumfrey was the senior partner of Henry Pumfrey & Son. I was then a recently appointed partner. At a partners meeting one evening one of the partners announced that one of our clients, Wates Limited, the builders and developers, had challenged us to a cricket match. Raymond Pumfrey who had a staccato way of speaking barked out "Huh, but nobody here can play cricket." There was a short silence broken by me saying "I haven't played much recently, but I have played county cricket." All the partners looked at me with new respect, especially the one who was a member of the M.C.C. "Which county did you play for Duncan?" Raymond Pumfrey barked out. "Merioneth" was my reply. "Where the hell is that?" asked Raymond Pumfrey. "It's in Wales" I responded, quickly realising that my new found status was swiftly and surely slipping away. In fact I only ever played one game for Merioneth and I believe that was because of a fixture mix up over a bank holiday when all the regular players had gone away. I did take one wicket though before the game was rained off. At the time Flintshire had made some 80 runs and had not lost any wickets so things were not going well for Merioneth.

In any event we did play Wates at cricket and, if I recall correctly, were well beaten. However we got better and thereafter gave them a real game once a year. When the firm merged with J.D.Langton & Passmore we found that they played cricket too and we were now able to field a reasonable side.

168

One of our female partners had a weekend cottage in the pretty village of Swinbrook in the Cotswolds and she challenged the village side to a game in what became a yearly fixture. The cricket ground was beautifully situated with on one side an attractive stretch of the river Windrush and a fine village pub called "The Swan Inn". On some occasions we made a weekend of it and then we usually played another law firm on the Saturday and the village team on the Sunday. The matches were often quite close and always hard fought. If it was a weekend fixture our team stayed at the riverside inn which was highly enjoyable. If we won we had a few beers to celebrate our victory and if we lost we had a few beers to drown our sorrows. These matches provided a very pleasant break from office life.

On one occasion we were challenged to a game of cricket by J.H.Kenyon Limited, the funeral directors, who were also clients of ours. This match though took place not at Swinbrook but just North of Hampstead. The Northern side of the ground was bordered by Hampstead cemetery and, as we went to inspect the pitch, I was aware of the rows of graves lying on slightly higher land at right angles to the pitch. I turned to the managing director of our clients and said "I see that your supporters have already arrived." This attempt at humour I am sorry to say fell rather flat. I suspect the directors of the company were allergic to this type of joke. All I can now recall of this match was bowling slow off spinners to the same managing director. The director never hit the ball, but I never hit the wicket, so honours were broadly even.

Another activity which I thoroughly enjoyed was the annual partners walk. When Stonehams & Pumfreys merged with J.D.Langton & Passmore we were told that J.D.Langton & Passmore had a sailing sub-committee and a walking sub-committee. I was no yachtsman, but I did enjoy walking so I became a regular on the annual office walk. I believe that with partners from both of the old firms taking part we got to know each other very much better than would otherwise have been the case. Because of the difficulty of finding accommodation in the countryside, the group was always restricted to six partners and of these three or four were regulars. We used to drive to some village inn on a Thursday night and typically walk 16 miles on the Friday, 16 miles on the Saturday and eight miles on the Sunday before driving home.

Until I took over the planning, the office walks were led by Michael Borne who as well as being a solicitor was also an archaeologist. Among our group of walkers we also had an ornithologist, a botanist, a railway buff (who could also recite all the Stanley Holloway monologues about Albert - the lad with the stick with a horse's head handle who in one poem was eaten by a lion) and a classicist who could read all the Latin inscriptions. I had no particular expertise so I read up all the guide books in advance and would give out regular nuggets of information such as explaining that Hardy's Monument in Dorset was not put up to commemorate the writer Thomas Hardy as many believe, but rather to honour the other Thomas Hardy famed in the battle of Trafalgar for being affectionately addressed by Nelson as he, Nelson, lay dying. Spike Milligan told a good, but irreverent, joke about Nelson's death: he said that when he, Spike, was going around HMS Victory he saw a plaque sticking out from the deck which read "Nelson fell here." I am not surprised" said Spike "I nearly tripped over the darned thing myself." Dorset was a favourite county for our walks, but we also walked in Devon, Somerset, Wiltshire, Hampshire, the Isle of Wight and over two years we covered most of the Cotswold Way.

I well recall the first office walk I went on which was in Dorset. The walks always took place in March and whatever the weather I always wore shorts. I believe that we started our walk at Dorchester. We had not been walking for very long

170

and were close to Maiden Castle, an Iron Age hill fort, when it started to snow. We stopped and sat on some abandoned agricultural machinery and one of my partners produced some corn beef sandwiches made with ryvita which he shared around. I sat there in my shorts, shivering and thinking that I could be in a nice warm office eating ham sandwiches made with crusty bread. I never told my kind partner that I did not like corn beef or ryvita as he was being very generous. In fact the weather then got better and never again on our walks did we have to contend with snow.

At the end of an interesting day's walk we arrived at a small village called Piddletrenthide where we stayed the night at a splendid pub called "The Poachers Inn". After taking off our rucksacks, we were all making short work of pints of bitter when I heard a customer say "Can I have a whisky and piddle please?" I assumed that I must have misheard, but another customer went up to the bar and said the same thing. My curiosity aroused I approached the bar and spoke to the landlord who happened to be a Yorkshireman. "What is a whisky and piddle?" I asked. "A whisky and water" he said in his Yorkshire accent. The landlord then went on to explain that the village was situated on the river Piddle and that was where his tap water came from. The landlord had carefully prepared labels stating that the contents were "genuine piddle water", put them on empty tonic water bottles and filled them up from the tap. "The locals don't tend to order them" he said "but the Americans love them." An enterprising and canny man from Yorkshire he surely was.

The partner who supplied us with the corn beef sandwiches, one Ralph Thompson, was a somewhat eccentric character who was liked by everybody. Ralph had a strong sense of morality and his language was always temperate. One year he was, as usual, on our annual walk when we were working our way through a thick forest near Mere in

Wiltshire. It was raining heavily and we were all soaked to the skin and none too happy. We stopped to have a rest and through a gap in the trees we could see a tall tower. This was King Alfred's Tower, a 160 foot high folly built in 1772. Ralph Thompson to try and encourage us said with a smile "Cheer up and remember chaps that this is all character forming." We then set off and walked for a miserable hour. The forest was dark, wet and very dense. Suddenly we spotted a break in the trees. We could see something looming. It was King Alfred's Tower and what was worse it was the same view that we had seen before. We had walked in a complete circle. Ralph Thompson for the only time I knew him lost it; he said "Bugger character forming!" and sat down distraught.

On our drive home from one of our walking trips I suggested that we play pub cricket. Ralph Thompson did not know the game and I explained that you had to look out for pub signs and count the legs that the name suggested. For example "The Coach and Horses" must contain at least eight legs and thus you would score eight runs. On the other hand "The Cross Keys" would have no legs and you would be out. There were four of us in the car and Ralph was driving. Suddenly Ralph would see a pub sign up a side road and he would excitedly point at the sign and say "It's 'The Crown', you are out." Unfortunately this and other similar instances was accompanied by a violent swerve. In the end Ralph's white faced passengers had to kill the game before Ralph killed them. I don't think Ralph ever discovered why we did not wish to carry on playing pub cricket with him ever again. A really great character was Ralph.

As mentioned when Michael Borne gave up planning the walks I took over. The first walk I organised was from Dulverton in Somerset to the Valley of the Rocks in Devon. It was a great walk and we had fine weather. On our first day we had lunch at a pretty thatched pub in Winsford called "The

Royal Oak". After lunch we were climbing up a steep hill when one of my younger partners who was at the rear of the group saw a fifty pound note lying on the ground which he promptly picked up. Now in those days fifty pound notes were somewhat rare - and somewhat valuable. One of the older partners, seeing this said "I think that must be mine, I thought I might have a hole in my pocket." "What's the serial number?" my younger partner quickly responded. Despite the fact that the older man did not know the answer, my younger partner had very reluctantly to hand the note over. From joy to despair in a flash.

On this same walk I recall the party split at one point when three intrepid walkers waded across a river leaving the other three, including me, on the other side. Later we thought we caught sight of Ralph Thompson on the top of a far off hill, but a view through binoculars established that it was in fact the back end of a grazing donkey! We finally met up with the breakaway group at "The Rising Sun" a picturesque inn in Lynmouth on the Devon coast where we were spending the night. The others had got to the inn first and as it was getting dark they were concerned at our late arrival. We had in fact been walking along a treacherous path that ran beside the river Lyn. During the winter large chunks of the path had fallen into the river and I as leader was somewhat anxious as I did not want any of us to follow them in. However we got through safely, although by the time we reached Lynmouth it was quite dark. Ralph, by the way, was not amused at being mistaken for a donkey seen from whatever end.

The Cotswold Way which I had planned for us to walk over two years was badly affected by really awful weather in the first year. We decided to abort the walk mid-day on the Saturday because of torrential rain. It was just not any fun at all. The next year we started some ten or so miles back from where we should have been and thus we never reached the end of this long distance footpath. This was sadly our last office walk because the country was then hit by a longish recession and it just did not seem appropriate for six of the more senior partners to take a Friday off whilst their colleagues remained at the office working hard.

Long distance walking is something that I have enjoyed doing throughout my adult life. I have walked with my partners, with flatmates, with my wife and family and with my wife and other couples. I have walked Offa's Dyke Path, the Cleveland Way and the Coast to Coast Path as well as sections of other long distance paths such as the Pembrokeshire Coast Path, the Ridgeway and the Cotswold Way as already mentioned.

A strange coincidence occurred when I was walking Offa's Dyke Path. The walk which runs from Chepstow in the South to Prestatyn in the North broadly follows the English/Welsh border. Of course you can walk it North to South, but most walkers start at Chepstow. I calculate that with occasional diversions to find accommodation I walked in all just over 180 miles. I was walking on this occasion with my wife and my two stepsons and we had got as far as Fronccysllte, a small village near Llangollen, when my wife developed large blisters behind each knee. Carrying on which would have caused my wife agony when climbing the many stiles that lay ahead was not an option so she and her two sons took a train home. I though decided to carry on partly because I like finishing things when I have started them and partly because the next leg was to take me through some of the countryside where I was brought up. My walk began with the crossing of Telford's famous aqueduct - an exciting few minutes if like me you suffer from vertigo.

After about 18 miles I was in the Clwydian hills and it was getting quite dark. I was walking towards a stile and I could see a woman walking across a field on my left towards the same stile. We met and the woman who was a local farmer's wife asked me what I was doing out there. I said that I was walking Offa's Dyke Path. "Where are you going to stay overnight?" she asked. I said that I intended to try and hitchhike into Ruthin which was some four miles away. "But that's off the Path" she retorted. I then explained that I had been brought up in Ruthin and was keen to revisit it as I had not been there for many years. "Where in Ruthin did you live?" was the next question. I told her the name of our house which was Plas Coch and she said "But that's where Jimmy Duncan lived." This to me was not all that surprising because my father who had a farm in the Clwydian hills would have been well known to other farmers in the area. I explained that I was in fact Jimmy Duncan's son. The woman's next comment though threw me entirely. "He was in the local paper last weekend" she said. "You must be mistaken" I answered "because he died twenty years ago." The woman, however, maintained that what she said was right and promised to send me the cutting from the local paper, which she duly did. On reading this on my return home I found out that Heinz Werth, an ex-German prisoner of war had just visited the Ruthin area and had told the reporter that he had been there before as a prisoner of war when he had worked on Jimmy Duncan's farm. It was a strange coincidence that I should be in the area at the same time as my late father's name appeared in the local newspaper and something of which I would have been unaware if the paths of the farmer's wife and I had not crossed and we had not had that particular conversation.

I cannot honestly say that I remember Heinz Werth but I do recall both German and Italian prisoners of war working on our farm at the end of the war. I would have been about nine or ten and I found the prisoners of war very interesting people to talk to and I could not relate to them as enemies. The prisoners wore an outfit rather like pyjamas and there were red circles, if I recall correctly, behind their knees and in the centre of their backs. I asked my father what these circles were for and he explained that if the prisoners tried to run away they were first shot in their knees and, if they persisted, then in their backs. I thought at the time, and still do, that this was very unsporting. Not in the British tradition.

Another office venture I recall was when the firm had a share of a box at the Goodwood racecourse near Chichester in Sussex. I remember one of the partners coming up with the idea at a partners meeting. The cost to me seemed very reasonable and I recall somewhat facetiously saying "I suppose therefore that it faces the wrong way." In fact it did! To see the race one had to leave the box entirely or watch it on a television screen. After a while though watching it on screen when the actual race was taking place just outside seemed quite normal. The food supplied was excellent and it was a stunning location to entertain clients. The sweep of the South Downs on which the racecourse lay was magnificent. As the Goodwood Estate was a client of the firm we also had on our first visit a tour of Goodwood House which was a splendid building with fine furnishings and paintings - the Canalettos were particularly worth seeing. I am not a great racing fan, but I have read that Goodwood is one of the most beautiful racecourses in the world and having been there I can certainly believe it.

As well as Goodwood the firm also once had an outing to Audley End House which is situated just outside Saffron Walden where we had an office. We acted for the Braybrooke family who used to own the estate before English Heritage took over and I have a memory of the heir to the title driving a miniature steam train around the grounds with the entire firm from the senior partner to the most junior secretary following on behind seated on blocks with their legs dangling on either

176

side. A sight to behold indeed. This stately home also had Canalettos which were also well worth seeing.

A venture which had limited success was the opera club which I started. I would select something from the English National Opera programme which looked interesting and then invite members of the firm to buy tickets. Now looking back I can only remember one opera-going occasion, but it did stand out. It was a double programme. First was "The Seven Deadly Sins" by Kurt Weill with libretto by Bertolt Brecht followed by "Les Mamelles de Tiresias" composed by Francis Poulenc. I think only four of us decided to attend this unusual theatrical treat. They were the then senior partner, a secretary, a young articled clerk and myself. The first opera involved Anna, played by an opera singer and a dancer at the same time, being tempted by the seven deadly sins. The second opera was centred on a woman who becomes a man. Therese/Tiresias had one red balloon and one green balloon to represent each breast and these float upwards at the point of transition. I found both operas fascinating and I enjoyed the contrasting music, but this was the articled clerk's first experience of opera and I can see him now with a dropped jaw and a gaping mouth. To say he was struck dumb with shock would be broadly correct. I hope this experience did not put our articled clerk off opera for life, but I fear it may have done. In any event the opera club did not recover and that was, as far as I can remember, its last visit to the Coliseum.

During my spell in Mayfair we used to have each year a grand Christmas lunch at the Naval and Military club. On one occasion I organised a quiz. One section involved guessing the names of London tube stations from cryptic clues which I set. My favourite clues were: "designed part of a funeral habit; a card game played at a round table; and what Dick Turpin did." The answers were - of course? - Maida Vale; Knightsbridge; and Blackhorse Road. I have, as mentioned before, always enjoyed puns so this was fertile territory for my twisted mind. When Stoneham Langton & Passmore merged with Bircham & Co I was pleased to discover that Birchams also had splendid Christmas lunches for the partners. Birchams also have a fine tradition of inviting former partners to lunch at Christmas - a great chance to catch up with what is going on in the legal world and to reminisce with old friends.

Other miscellaneous office activities that I can recall were football matches - I played rugby at school and was hopeless at soccer, so I normally supported from the touchlines - darts matches and chess matches. Netball matches were of course for ladies only save on one occasion near the beginning of my career that I recall when the younger girls in the office, who played in a league asked the men in the firm to play against them so as to give them practice of playing against taller players. I was one of the male players involved and I must say that I did feel rather foolish playing netball in Lincoln's Inn Fields whilst observed by curious and somewhat uncomprehending spectators. This though was compounded when a hooligan passing by for no good reason, save perhaps that he had had too much to drink at lunch, assaulted one of the male players in our team and broke his rather expensive glasses As a consequence we all ended up at the police station in Holborn. "And you were doing what?" said the sergeant, looking askance when I said that we had all been playing netball. The sergeant seemed even more taken aback when he found out that the men who were all dressed in t-shirts and shorts were actually lawyers in a nearby law firm.

Overall the activities that I have described were thoroughly enjoyable and they have provided me with a lot of happy memories. I had a social life away from the firm, but these firm related social events were a bonus that was well worth having.

CHAPTER TEN

Employment Tribunals

In the summer of 1994, when I was just under four years from retiring as a partner in my law firm (we had compulsory retirement at 62), I took my first step to provide myself with further work after leaving private practice. I applied to what is now called the Ministry of Justice and was in due course appointed as a part time chairman of the industrial tribunals. By the time I had retired from this post the title was employment judge of the employment tribunals and for convenience I shall hereafter use this term. Employment judges, who must be either barristers or solicitors of at least seven years standing, usually sit with two lay members, one being appointed to the post after consultation with an employers organisation (e.g. the CBI) and one after consultation with an employees organisation (e.g. the TUC).

The tribunal's jurisdiction primarily covers specific disputes arising out of employment or work and the parties are normally employers, employees or workers, trade unions and the State. "Workers" includes employees and others who provide personal services under a contract such as freelance workers or self-employed workers. Suffice to say the question of whether a claimant is an employee or a worker is not always an easy one to answer and it can be critical because many employment rights (e.g. the right not to be unfairly dismissed) are only available to employees.

The most common types of case are unfair dismissal, discrimination and employment contract claims such as non-payment of wages. However employment tribunals also handle issues arising out of redundancy dismissals, maternity and paternity leave rights, flexible working rights, rights to take time off for care of dependants, for studies, for training,

179

or for union duties and rights under the Working Time Regulations 1998 such as the right to have daily rests, annual leave and pay during such. There are further miscellaneous rights of a rather different nature which include appeals against improvement and prohibition notices (relating to health and safety at work) and appeals against levy assessments by an Industrial Training Board.

Unlawful discrimination during my time as a judge has expanded greatly. Starting with sex (including equal pay claims) and race, legislation has added disability, religion or belief, sexual orientation and age. It is difficult to think of what more Brussels can come up with - obesity perhaps! The employment tribunal however only has jurisdiction over unlawful discrimination that occurs during employment or work. This includes discrimination against persons who are applying for jobs, persons in employment and contract workers.

Discrimination, namely choosing one of two or more options in its simplest form, is not of itself unlawful. It is the basis of the choice that can render it so. For example, if two applicants apply for a job and one is male and the other female, whichever is chosen must involve discrimination against the other. If however the choice is based on, for example, the qualifications held by the successful candidate and this is shown to be the case the other candidate will not be successful in any claim. The losing candidate though might believe that he or she was not chosen because the employer wanted a person of the other sex. If in those circumstances the losing candidate brings a claim she (let us say) will have to prove to the tribunal that the prospective employer "on the ground of her sex" treated her less favourably than the employer treated the man. The problem for employers seeking staff is that in the example I have given they could be faced with an unlawful discrimination claim whichever applicant they choose as the same provision applies to discrimination against men. Some claimants bring such cases because they feel that their merits should have got them the job in question, but they have no real evidence of any unlawful discrimination. On occasion though claimants may have some sort of an indication that unlawful discrimination is taking place. For example a male applicant waiting to go in to an interview after a female applicant is coming out might hear the chairman of the company say "what a pretty girl." Such evidence though in my experience is not that common. More often than not there is nothing clear cut and it is a matter for the tribunal to look at all the available facts and draw the appropriate inferences.

In the 14 years that I was involved with employment tribunals I sat as an employment judge on just short of 1200 days; I also spent about 30 days attending training sessions, about 10 days assisting in interviewing applicants who wished to be lay members and countless days writing up decisions, researching into the law relevant to the cases I was sitting on and keeping up to date with changes in employment law which during my period sitting in tribunals was a very regular occurrence. After I had retired as a solicitor I estimate that I probably spent on average half of each working week on tribunal work. Whilst I was still practising as a solicitor though I had obligations to my clients, but I still managed to average 45 sitting days per year; this number however increased dramatically when I was a free agent. There was a fairly constant need, at least in my region, for part time judges to sit and I was often rung up the day before and asked to sit at short notice. I did not mind this though because I enjoyed the job which was more often than not interesting and challenging. I felt that, although I had retired from full time work, I was still making a real contribution to society.

I was appointed to start sitting from 1 September 1994 and indeed had my first case on that very day. I was originally allocated to sit in Central London, but later on I was transferred to London East which also covered the whole of East Anglia. Sittings thereafter took place at Stratford in the East End of London, at Norwich in Norfolk and at Bury St Edmunds in Suffolk.

In 1998, about a month before I was due to retire as a partner in my law firm, my wife and I moved from Belsize Park in North London to a house close to Nayland in Suffolk which was just over the Essex border and in the beautiful Stour valley. This made sense if I was to continue sitting in East London and East Anglia, as was my intention. Nevertheless I still had to cope with some fairly lengthy journeys - unless that is I was sitting at Bury St Edmunds which I could reach by car in about 45 minutes. At the end of 2004 my wife and I moved to a house near Orford which was deeper into Suffolk and nearer to the coast. My journey time from my home to Stratford was now just over two hours, to Norwich about one and a half hours and to Bury St Edmunds just over one hour. This made for some long working days, particularly in the winter if there was any snow on rail or road to hold things up. Then a day sitting at Stratford could easily include a 5 hours commute.

Assuming that I was allocated to sit on a short and relatively straightforward case of unfair dismissal in Stratford a typical day in the latter years of my career would be as follows. I would get up at 6.15 a.m., leave the house at 7 a.m. and arrive at the Stratford tribunal offices just after 9 a.m. I would then have under an hour to look at the file, read the claim (the document setting out details of the claim) and the response (the document setting out details of the defence) and check on any unusual legal issues arising. I would go into court at about 9.50 a.m. so as to greet my lay members and to brief them on what to look out for. The court hearing would start at 10 a.m. and I would first clarify with the parties what were the key issues in the case that had to be decided. We would then usually hear the employer's main witness first. Normally evidence would be given from a written statement and the employee or his or her representative would then ask questions (cross examination). We, the tribunal members, would then put any questions we had. The employer or his or her representative would then ask questions arising out of the cross examination or our questions (re-examination). This procedure would then be repeated for each further witness and the same procedure would then apply to the employee and his or her witnesses. Finally the employee's side would give reasons why the employee should succeed and then the employer's side would give reasons why the employer should succeed (submissions). I and my two colleagues would then withdraw and consider our decision in private.

Coming to a decision involved first of all agreeing what the key issues were. Secondly, my colleagues and I would establish what the relevant facts were that would enable us to reach a decision. Where there was a dispute over what had happened, a not unusual situation, we would have to decide which version of the facts put forward was to be accepted. Thirdly I would then advise my lay members as to the relevant law. Fourthly we would formulate our conclusions and in the example I have given decide whether there was an unfair dismissal or not.

In the course of reaching a decision with my lay members I would make notes of what I wished to say and then on our return to court I would give the tribunal's decision which required me to explain how my colleagues and I had reached our conclusions. During this the tape recorder was running. Generally my tribunal would reach a unanimous decision, but there were occasions when one member took a different view to the other two. In theory the two lay members could out vote the legal member, but this never happened to me. In any event the majority vote prevailed. If the tribunal decided the case in favour of the employer that would normally be it, but if we found in favour of the employee we would hear further evidence (if we had not heard it already) with regard to the remedy the claimant was seeking. Keeping to my example the claimant might want reinstatement or compensation for losses incurred by him or her because of the dismissal. In such a case we would then repeat the process and eventually give a decision as to remedy. I, and I am sure this applies to my colleagues as well, did my best to do all this in one day, but it would often require a further hearing day to bring matters to a conclusion. Generally we would finish between 4 p.m. and 4.30 p.m. but it could be much later. The lay members would then go home, but I would stay on and usually check through decisions that the typists had typed up, make amendments and sign off the final versions. I would then leave round about 5 p.m. and get home just after 7 p.m. It was a long, albeit usually satisfying, day.

Identifying the key issues in any case, whether simple or complicated, is an extremely important part of the judicial process. The key issues are in effect the questions that have to be answered by the court so that it can determine the claim on a logical basis. For example in an unfair dismissal case the key issues might be:

1. Was the claimant an employee at the time of the alleged dismissal?
2. Has the claimant been employed for a continuous period of not less than one year?
3. Was the claimant actually dismissed?
4. Was the true reason for dismissal misconduct as the employer alleges?
5. Was the dismissal fair?
6. What remedy is the claimant entitled to?

184

As it is only employees who have been employed for a continuous period of not less than one year who have the right not to be unfairly dismissed it will be seen that to have any chance of success the claimant must get the tribunal to give affirmative answers to the first three questions above, whereas thereafter the employer will only succeed if the tribunal answers the next two questions in the affirmative; the sixth question of course will only need to be answered if the claimant wins his or her case.

The reader who does not have any experience of employment tribunals may possibly consider it odd that the question of whether there had been a dismissal was one of the key issues in the example I gave above. In fact this question cropped up more often than one might expect. An interesting example occurred in a reported case called Futty v D & D Brekkes Ltd. Mr Futty worked as a fish filleter for D & D Brekkes Ltd. One day Mr Futty's foreman, who was not impressed with Mr Futty's attitude, said to him "if you do not like the job, fuck off." Mr Futty left the premises, did not return to work and got himself another job. Mr Futty then claimed that he had been dismissed and brought a claim for unfair dismissal. The employers however denied that they had dismissed Mr Futty and said that they assumed that he would return to work after getting over his tantrum. After hearing evidence of what usually went on around the fish dock, the tribunal held (perhaps surprisingly) that the words used by the foreman were not words of dismissal, but a general encouragement to Mr Futty to get on with his job. Accordingly Mr Futty's claim failed. Of course there might well have been a different result if the background circumstances had been different. What goes in a fish dock might not be seen in the same light in say a hairdressing salon. Futty the fish filleter who was told to fuck off does sound too good to be true, but as his story appears in a reported case the alliteration must be purely accidental.

185

Deciding issues of fact was often an important part of the decision making process. Friends who are not lawyers have often asked me how I and my lay members were able to decide which witnesses were telling the truth and to what extent we relied on the body language of witnesses. Looking back I find it difficult to recall any case where the witness's body language was determinative in helping us reach a particular conclusion. It is in any event, particularly where the witness comes from a different culture, a somewhat uncertain guide. What, for example, may look like shiftiness could simply be the witness showing deference to the court.

More often than not I found that witnesses who were lying would give themselves away. Sometimes a letter or email would be sent by a witness at the relevant time that was either inconsistent with the factual situation that the witness alleged existed or was silent on the subject when one would expect it to be mentioned. For example if a male employee was complaining of homophobic remarks made to him by work colleagues I would consider it very odd if the next day he sent a letter to his father telling him what had occurred and then set out a different set of allegations when he came to put in his claim; or if a female employee who was alleging that on a specific date she had been sexually harassed by a colleague the next day sent a letter to her manager complaining about the lack of heating in her office, but failed to mention the harassment. In the first case I would need some persuading that the description of what had taken place set out in the claim was more reliable than the version the claimant gave to his father shortly after the event. In the second case I could appreciate that there might be a good reason for the omission in the letter, but I would require the witness to explain why she had failed to mention the harassment and I would then consider whether the explanation she gave was credible or not.

Sometimes a witness would be caught out lying about some things that were not of crucial importance to the success or failure of the claim. My tribunal might then conclude that this propensity to lie showed that the witness could not be trusted when giving evidence that was essential to support the claim. An example of this was a claimant in one of the cases that I heard who claimed that he had a law degree, but later was forced to admit that he had not even finished the course. This together with other lies that the claimant had told led my tribunal to conclude that the claimant was not a reliable witness and, as we did not have similar reservations about the employers' evidence, we rejected his claim.

On it appeared to me a surprisingly large number of occasions witnesses would contradict themselves. This particularly occurred where the witness had read out to the court his or her witness statement - a document, if their side was represented, that was usually prepared by a solicitor. During cross examination the witness in answering questions would then, no doubt forgetting the prepared case, give evidence that was in some respects contrary to their own witness statement. In such instances, particularly where the discrepancies were critical to the success or failure of the case, my colleagues and I might conclude that the witness was lying – more probably in the witness statement than in their oral evidence. Of course there were occasions when it was much harder to determine which side was telling the truth, but normally there was some clue, however small, that would assist the tribunal in deciding where the truth lay. I have read of judges in criminal cases who have found it very difficult to determine who was telling the truth and I suspect that the relative ease I had in this area was solely due to the fact that I was determining employment disputes where there was nearly always an abundance of paper evidence unlike criminal cases, save for fraud and suchlike, where paperwork was limited.

Unfair dismissal cases could be relatively straightforward, but many of these and nearly all discrimination cases had some complications. It was not an uncommon occurrence to hear evidence of how a particular employee had carried out his or her duties or had suffered what they claimed was unlawful discrimination over lengthy periods of time (a year or more was by no means unusual). If the claimant relied on a number of different events to prove his or her case, the tribunal might well hear a large number of witnesses as different people might well have been present on each occasion. The relevant documents in the bundle prepared by the parties could easily number over a hundred pages and could in the more complex cases run into thousands. Sometimes evidence was given of a number of disciplinary hearings, each one of them lasting some hours. Notes of such hearings were regularly taken by the employer and occasionally the employee would have a note taken; it was then odds on that there would be disputes over what had actually been said at these meetings. Matters such as these naturally all added to the length of the tribunal hearings.

Over the 14 years that I sat in the employment tribunals the longest case that I ever tried was scheduled to last 34 days, but in fact I was able to conclude it in 26 days, having lost the other eight days for one reason or another as the case was progressing. The decision in that case was reserved, namely given in writing at a later date. The decision with extended reasons covered 35 pages of A4. On the other hand there were occasions when four cases could be dealt with in one day, but that was very much the exception. Sometimes the parties would settle at the last minute - not an unusual occurrence - and a three day case could then be concluded in under half an hour. If I was sitting at Stratford there would nearly always be "a floater" or two waiting to be heard. "Floaters" were cases listed to be heard on the particular day but not allocated to a particular court. Accordingly the parties had to wait for another case to finish hopefully early enough for their case to be heard and concluded. In Bury St Edmunds if I finished early I would usually be able pick up another judge's case. If I was sitting at Norwich, which was just a sitting centre with no attendant back up staff, there were no floaters and if a case finished early it would mean the end to my day in court. Considering the time it took for me to get there and back I always found this an irritating waste of my time and an undue cost to the State.

When I was still in practice as a solicitor I usually sat on one day cases, because I also had my clients' affairs to attend to and did not wish to be away from my office for more than one day at a time. When I retired from practice though I could and did take on multi-day cases. One day cases were usually allocated the day before the hearing and thus, unless I was sitting in the same location the day before and could take home the relevant papers to read overnight, I had, as I have already explained, to read them up on the day. If I was sitting at Norwich or at Bury St Edmunds the practice was to send the relevant papers by post, but this could only be of benefit if their listing clerk knew in advance that I would be sitting there as I left home long before the post arrived.

Multi-day cases were generally allocated in advance, but sometimes cases had to be switched from one judge to another (e.g. because the judge knew one of the parties or had fallen ill overnight) and then one had to familiarise oneself with the case with limited time available. However when you regularly have less than an hour to read the case papers you soon develop a technique which allows you to ascertain the key issues very quickly. It is not perhaps an ideal situation but it seems to work. Certainly in the course of time one's powers of concentration become well honed.

The longer cases were usually, but not always, the more interesting. Certainly the longer cases required constant concentration. I might mention at this point that I have heard the public criticize judges for working a short day. Those who criticize do not I suspect realise the level of concentration that is required. One has to listen attentively to all of the evidence and take as near as possible a written note of everything that is said. Written witness statements have of course helped, but it is not unusual for somebody representing themselves to turn up without a witness statement in which event, unless they are directed to go away and prepare one, everything they say has to be carefully written down by the judge. Evidence given under cross examination or re-examination which by its very nature cannot be written down in advance has likewise to be carefully recorded. This can in a complicated case easily last several hours or sometimes even days. Cramp in the hands is not unknown and backache is almost an integral part of the job.

I believe that five to five and a half hours sitting in court is quite long enough, as after that however hard one tries one's concentration can waver; further the "homework" (research into the law, keeping up to date with developments in the law, writing decisions, checking draft decisions) has to be added on and this "extra time" is often I believe disregarded by the critics. There are though occasions where it is preferable to sit late so that a case can be finished rather than adjourned to a date which may often be some months ahead. In such situations, with the agreement of the parties, their representatives, if any, and the lay members, I have occasionally sat beyond 6 p.m., but it is not something that I think should be done regularly. The real problem here is that, if a case is adjourned, it is usually very difficult to find an early date that is available to the tribunal, the representatives, the parties and the witnesses.

Adjournments for over three months were unfortunately by no means unusual. Such a gap is clearly not satisfactory for anybody and especially not for a dismissed employee who had failed to find another job. If, as would normally be the case, I had sat on many other hearings in the meantime it was not always easy to keep in mind one's feel of the adjourned case, despite having written notes of the evidence given up to the date of the adjournment. My practice therefore was also to jot down my initial views of those witnesses that had given their evidence and how such evidence might impact on the key issues. Adjournments occurred more often than in a perfect world should have been the case. In my experience this was not normally because the tribunal was slow in bringing the case to a conclusion, but more often than not because the representatives or the unrepresented parties had been very optimistic in indicating at an earlier stage how long the case would take. This was the basis on which the tribunal administration had determined the number of days that would be required to conclude the case and was usually outside the control of the sitting judge. It should be noted that one could not just add a day on to the days fixed, because of other commitments that the judge, lay members, representatives and witnesses would have. There of course also had to be a court room available and in Stratford during my time they were normally all in use.

Once a decision had been given that was usually the end of it from the point of view of the judge, but not always. A dissatisfied party could apply for a review on certain grounds (e.g. that new evidence had become available that could not have been reasonably known of or foreseen at the time of the hearing) which if successful could result in the tribunal rehearing the case; or on an appeal the appeal court might remit the case back to the same tribunal to rehear it or the appeal court might require the judge to answer certain questions as to matters that were not contained in the decision.

Having described how the employment tribunal system operated and how I managed to cope with the various problems that I encountered, I shall now revisit some of the cases that I presided over which I believe were either factually or legally interesting and which I hope will prove to be of some interest to the reader.

The case of Hall v Woolston Hall Leisure Limited was, of interest because of a legal point of some importance that emerged somewhat unexpectedly. It all started in January 1996 when my tribunal began hearing Mrs Hall's case of unlawful sex discrimination. Unfortunately we could not finish the case on that day and we fixed a further hearing in May 1996 which was the first date available to all. Mrs Hall, an experienced chef, employed by a limited company at a golf club in Epping Forest, was told by the managing director of the limited company that she was being made redundant. At the time Mrs Hall was pregnant and she contended that this was the real reason for her dismissal - thus sex discrimination. My tribunal found in favour of Mrs Hall but regrettably there was again insufficient time left to conclude matters and the case was further adjourned to a date in November 1996.

Mrs Hall was seeking compensation for loss of wages and injury to her feelings. When we all reassembled in November 1996 Mrs Hall to support her claim for loss of wages gave evidence that each week her employers gave her £250 in notes and a pay slip. I asked Mrs Hall if she had any pay slips with her and she produced some which showed gross pay of £250.00, deductions of £63.35 and a net sum paid of £186.65. Mrs Hall said that, when she queried the way her wages were being paid, the managing director said "it's the way we do business." Having heard this evidence I queried whether the employers had been paying all the tax due on Mrs Hall's wages to the Inland Revenue. After taking instructions the barrister who was representing the limited company, with some understandable embarrassment, contended that, as the way in which his clients were performing the contract of employment was unlawful, the contract was therefore tainted with illegality. Accordingly the barrister submitted that, as the law would prohibit Mrs Hall from going to court to enforce the contract whilst she was still employed e.g. to recover unpaid wages, she had no legal rights that were destroyed when the contract was brought to an end. My tribunal with reluctance accepted the barrister's contention and it made no award for Mrs Hall's loss of wages from her dismissal onwards, but we considered that her claim for injury to feelings did not depend on the contract of employment, whether illegally performed or not, and we awarded Mrs Hall £2000 and interest thereon for the injury to her feelings.

Mrs Hall, who had so far been represented by a male friend, now instructed a barrister and she appealed to the Employment Appeal Tribunal. After a hearing in February 1998 judgment was given upholding our decision. At the end of the judgment the learned judge said that it was a basic principle of the administration of justice that the court would not permit a party to enforce an illegal contract that involved a fraud on the Revenue. The judge added that for the tribunal to award compensation for loss of earnings arising out of a contract of employment that was being performed illegally to the claimant's knowledge would breach that principle. Our decision was accordingly vindicated - but not as it turned out for long.

Undaunted Mrs Hall now instructed a Queen's Counsel as well as her previous barrister to pursue her case in the Court of Appeal. That court gave its judgment in May 2000 - five years after Mrs Hall's dismissal! The limited company was not represented in either appeal court, but in the Court of Appeal a barrister represented the State because of the importance to the public of the point in issue. The three Court of Appeal judges agreed with each other and, after considering the basic principles set out in a case decided in 1775, they analysed the more recent cases on illegal performance of contracts. The three judges concluded firstly that Mrs Hall's acquiescence in her employers' illegal performance of the contract was in no way causally linked with her sex discrimination claim and should not therefore lead to her forfeiting her claim to damages for any financial loss and secondly that the illegal performance of the contract would not render the contract unenforceable unless, in addition to knowledge of the facts which make the performance illegal, the employee actively participated in the illegal performance. The Court concluded that Mrs Hall did not herself actively participate in her employer's unlawful scheme and that on both grounds she was entitled to pursue her claim for loss of wages from her dismissal onwards. The case was therefore remitted back to my tribunal to make a further award.

As it happened my tribunal never did meet to decide what further compensation Mrs Hall was entitled to, because the limited company had financial problems and it became, as I understand it, likely that it would be unable to satisfy any tribunal award. I hope nevertheless that Mrs Hall recovered her initial award of £2000 plus, but it is I fear possible that Mrs Hall never recovered any money at all after her five year long legal battle.

The Court of Appeal decision in Mrs Hall's case has since become a leading authority on how illegality in its performance can affect employment contracts.

The case of Silva v Sense which took up four tribunal days was an example of a case that involved a fairly large number of facts and a great many documents (over a thousand) even though the major incidents covered a period of just ten months. Mr Silva who was born in Sri Lanka was employed

194

by the charity to look after disabled people at the charity's group homes. In November 1997 Mr Silva then aged 30 was dismissed because of misconduct and lack of capability to do his job. Mr Silva however claimed that his dismissal was both unfair and also an act of racial discrimination. Sense contended amongst other things that Mr Silva had arranged for a resident to shower whilst another was having a bath nearby and that he had brought a magazine called "Asian Babes" into work with the result that one of the residents saw it. Sense then contended that the reason why Mr Silva was dismissed was because he had sworn at a lady colleague, had repeatedly failed to pull up the trousers of a resident when they had fallen down and that on a resident's visit to a dentist he, seemingly not knowing the correct technique for folding and unfolding a wheelchair, had taken the wheels off, thereby possibly putting the safety of the resident at risk. Mr Silva did not really dispute these allegations, but contended that he was singled out because of his race and that others who had behaved in a similar fashion had not been dismissed. Our tribunal though considered that Mr Silva's contentions had to be considered in the context of a history of complaints about his performance over a number of years and we decided that, although the dismissal itself was unfair because of procedural errors, it was not an act of race discrimination.

Mr Silva appealed to the Employment Appeal Tribunal against the decision. Mr Silva argued that the tribunal's decision was perverse. The notice of appeal was 10 pages long, backed up by a written argument of the same length containing 23 points that were said to be points of law. In giving judgment the Employment Appeal Tribunal commented on the enormous amount of material thrust upon both tribunals making it difficult to see the wood for the trees. The Employment Appeal Tribunal considered that the 23 points raised by Mr Silva did not relate to any points of law, save for an issue arising out of the calculation of the compensatory award. The Employment Appeal Tribunal held that what Mr Silva was actually doing was disputing the facts found by the tribunal as to which there is generally no right of appeal. However, apart from the small issue over the calculation of the compensatory award, the appeal did not succeed.

One unusual aspect of Mr Silva's original case and his appeal is that on both occasions he was represented by his sister who was a distinguished academic lawyer, but who the Employment Appeal Tribunal felt lacked experience in handling such an appeal. It is in my view a much harder task for a lay person to handle an appeal than present a claim and this case shows that both can in fact be difficult even for an academic lawyer.

Grayson v News Group Newspapers Limited was a particularly interesting case. It took up nine tribunal days between 26 August 1998 and 19 March 1999 and the decision was reserved and given on 13 April 1999. Mr Grayson, a photographer who was employed by the "News of the World" was dismissed in November 1997. Unhappy about this Mr Grayson brought a case of unfair dismissal.

The events leading up to Mr Grayson's dismissal really started with a coach trip of 20 Cornwall county councillors in October 1997. During that trip the councillors had spotted a wild animal akin to a puma which was known locally and elsewhere as "The Beast of Bodmin". Rebekah Wade, the acting editor of the "News of the World", thought this was a promising line of enquiry and on her instructions her subeditors dispatched two reporters and Mr Grayson to Cornwall and told them to come back with a good story. Ms Wade said that she wanted a light hearted piece and she suggested that the two reporters could dress up as Sherlock

196

Holmes and Doctor Watson and Mr Grayson could then photograph them as they were trying to track down the Beast.

The team took off for Cornwall on 21 October 1997 and Mr Grayson duly took photographs of the two reporters dressed up as instructed. On 23 October 1997 one of the reporters returned to London with the photographs and accompanying text. Ms Wade saw the material at an editorial conference but she was not impressed. Accordingly the now two man team were instructed to remain in Cornwall and carry out a proper investigation involving, for example, interviews with the councillors, views of an expert on big cats and photographs of places where sightings had occurred.

On 30 October 1997, nine days after their arrival in Cornwall, Mr Grayson and the remaining reporter contacted the newspaper and said that they had actually come across "The Beast of Bodmin" in the wild. Mr Grayson then wired the photographs through to the newspaper. Ms Wade was informed and she told her subeditors to tell the team that everybody had had a good laugh and if they now admitted that it was a stunt that would be an end of it. However the team stood by their story and Ms Wade then telephoned Mr Grayson who said that he was "pissed off" for getting a good story with pictures and then getting "a kick in the bollocks." Ms Wade, although still concerned about the authenticity of the story and the photographs, accepted what Mr Grayson had told her and decided to devote parts of the front page and four further inside pages to this scoop. Ms Wade also decided to arrange for TV interviews and an increase in the print run, which would be an initial expense to the newspaper. Mr Kuttner, the managing editor of the newspaper, at the request of Ms Wade then spoke to Mr Grayson and the reporter and challenged the truth of their story, but both employees explained how they had tracked the animal down and Mr

Grayson had photographed it. Mr Grayson added that he would not lie to his editor and his managing editor.

The following day, Friday 31 October 1997, Mr Grayson returned to London and saw Mr Kuttner in person. Mr Grayson again explained how they had come across the Beast in the wild and how he had photographed it before it ran away. Mr Grayson then saw Mr Kuttner at lunch time and Mr Grayson once again assured him that the story was true. Later the same day Ms Wade discovered that Mr Mahmood, the paper's senior investigative reporter who was a friend of Mr Grayson, knew nothing of the scoop and this made her suspicious. Ms Wade accordingly asked Mr Mahmood to ring Mr Grayson and check it out. Mr Mahmood rang Mr Grayson on two occasions and each time Mr Grayson stuck to his story. However Mr Mahmood thought that Mr Grayson was lying and told Ms Wade so. Ms Wade then rang Mr Grayson who after some prevarication finally admitted that the story and the photographs were fabrications. Mr Grayson said that the team were put under pressure to get a photograph of the Beast and it had been insinuated that they should "stunt" one.

It later appeared that Mr Grayson and the remaining reporter had gone to Dartmoor Wildlife Park where Mr Grayson had taken a number of pictures of a large puma through the bars of its enclosure to make it appear that it was running free. The story of coming across the Beast in the wild and how it had run away when it saw them was then made up by Mr Grayson and the reporter.

After an investigatory meeting and a disciplinary meeting Mr Grayson was dismissed on grounds of misconduct.

Mr Grayson's main argument before my tribunal was in effect that it was the common practice of the "News of the World" to fabricate stories and that as others had not been sacked for doing so neither should he be. When the case came to court Mr Grayson relied on seven stories that had been reported in the "News of the World" which he contended had fabrications in them. The tribunal was given the appropriate cuttings and then heard evidence of how the stories were obtained.

A witness of particular interest was Mr Mahmood (subsequently dubbed the "fake sheikh") who was accompanied by a large bodyguard called "Jaws." When giving evidence Mr Mahmood was permitted not to give his personal address as is usual for a witness, because he had explained that there was a contract out on his life. We also heard evidence from Rebekah Wade, the acting editor, and Mr Kuttner, the managing editor, of the "News of the World", but not from Rupert Murdoch himself.

The most intriguing evidence concerned the seven stories which Mr Grayson claimed had been fabricated or contained fabrications. After hearing the evidence though my tribunal came to the following conclusions on each newspaper article.

"Country Vice" was a story about prostitutes in rural areas. One of them was pictured in a large hat with a stalk of corn in her mouth - clearly a posed picture. The text stated that she was discovered by the reporter at a village called Locking Stumps. This was too good to be true. In fact it was not true as the reporter had taken her there from the neighbouring area where she actually worked. Apart from this and a suggestion that the name the woman gave was not her correct name (not really surprising in a prostitute), there was no criticism of the rest of the piece.

"Monopoly Mo" was a story about a gangster. There were accompanying photographs and the contention was that the pictures had been posed, but not so captioned. The evidence was though unclear and my tribunal did not find any real evidence of fabrication.

"News of the World Smashes SAS Machine Gun Racket" was a story about the sale and purchase of a machine gun. The gun was described as capable of firing 500 rounds per minute, but as the firing pin was missing my tribunal considered that this was misleading. We also considered the headline to be highly exaggerated, but we were not persuaded that the story itself was untrue or that the accompanying photograph of the seller had been posed.

"Community Service" was a story about a convicted person who made a mockery of his community service by going to the site where he was due to work in a Rolls Royce (which he did apparently own) and drinking beer on the job. Mr Grayson contended that the story was set up and that the beer was provided by the "News of the World", but there was no evidence to support that contention. We did though conclude that a photograph of the convicted person sitting in the Rolls Royce with his feet up was a reconstruction rather than a photograph that was actually taken during a period of his community service.

"Invasion of the Birdy-Snatchers" was a story about turkey rustling. Mr Grayson, who himself took the accompanying photographs, contended that the whole story of a gang stealing turkeys was made up and that he later met up with the rustlers in a local pub. My tribunal however did not accept that Mr Grayson later met the men at the inn nor that this was anything other than a genuine raid.

"The Plot to Kill" was a story based on an agreement between Jaws, Mr Mahmood's bodyguard, and another man to kill Mr Mahmood for £5000. In fact Mr Mahmood had asked Jaws to make these arrangements so that in a sense it was a set up, but the fact still remained that the other man was prepared to go along with the plan.

"Ford Escort Girls" was a story about prostitutes in cars. Mr Grayson alleged that the pictures were stunted, but on examination of the cutting we noted that no pictures in fact accompanied the story so that this allegation had no substance.

Overall we found no evidence to suggest a culture of fabrication at the "News of the World" as Mr Grayson had suggested. Although we had criticisms of some of the stories, we did not find anything close to the deception that Mr Grayson himself was prepared to put forward which was a lie from beginning to end. In short Mr Grayson was not able to persuade us that his dismissal was unfair. So ended a case which was full of interest throughout.

Shodeke v Hill, The London Borough of Havering and Others is another case that I will not forget in a hurry. It was the action that I have previously referred to which lasted 26 days. Ms Shodeke presented her own case, Ms Sally Robertson, a barrister, represented Mr Hill (after Mr Hill had started by acting for himself) and Mr Robin Allen Q.C., a very experienced counsel in employment law cases, represented the London Borough of Havering and certain other respondents. In reciting what occurred I shall describe how each hearing day went as the case is a good example of the difficulties facing a judge in concluding a case in time.

Ms Shodeke worked for the London Borough of Havering for just over four years until she was dismissed on 30 January 1998. During her employment Ms Shodeke brought three actions in which she claimed that she had suffered race discrimination and after her dismissal a fourth action in which she claimed that she had suffered race discrimination and that she had been unfairly dismissed.

The action which was scheduled to last 34 days started on 11 October 1999 with Ms Shodeke applying for an adjournment to a date to be fixed in the following year. Ms Shodeke gave two reasons for her application. First Ms Shodeke said that she had to be at home on occasions to look after her father who was unwell and secondly that she wished to be legally represented as her union had withdrawn its support two weeks before and she had been unable to obtain the services of a solicitor in the meantime. Ms Shodeke had made similar applications before that had been refused and my tribunal refused this application too. We considered that as Ms Shodeke was not suggesting that her father could not fend for himself and that as there were four other siblings living in the London area this was insufficient reason to adjourn. With regard to legal assistance we considered that Ms Shodeke' s problem was more a matter of lack of funds and that as she had had six months notice of the hearing dates it was, bearing in mind the inconvenience and cost to the Respondents, preferable for the action to proceed.

Having lost her application for an adjournment, Ms Shodeke then requested that one of my lay members should stand down on the grounds that he knew the human resources manager of the London Borough and that the cases should be heard by another three member tribunal in the following year. Mr Allen however said that the manager knew the lay member by sight only and that it was not his intention to call her as a witness. My lay member said that he had had no business or personal contact with the human resources manager and that such knowledge that he had of her would not influence his decision in any way. In those circumstances the application was refused.

I was ready for the action to now proceed so we discussed the issues arising out of the four complaints and I then asked Ms Shodeke to hand up copies of her witness statement which

202

according to a direction given by a judicial colleague should have been exchanged with those of her opponents at least six weeks before. Ms Shodeke explained however that she had not prepared her witness statement because she had expected the cases to be adjourned. Mr Allen then produced three folders of relevant documents, but Ms Shodeke said that she had only had them for a short time, had not read them and had herself documents she wished to produce. Again a judicial direction had been ignored. It was now after 4 p.m. and, accepting the reality of the situation, I directed that Ms Shodeke could stay at home the next day to prepare her witness statement whilst the tribunal read the folders of documents. This was to save time later as when a document was referred to in evidence we would already be familiar with it. The folders contained 819 pages of documents and as more were added during the hearing by the end of the case I am reasonably sure that we had over 1000 pages to read and digest.

On 13 October 1999, having read solidly for five hours the day before, the tribunal was keen to get started. However Mr Allen indicated that he was concerned that Ms Shodeke was stressed and tired and possibly not in a fit state to proceed. Ms Shodeke accordingly applied for an adjournment because of the state of her health and with reluctance we agreed. We then spent the next four hours or so continuing with our reading of the relevant documents.

On 14 October 1999 which was a Thursday all parties sought an adjournment. Mr Allen said that the London Borough of Havering was negotiating a settlement with Ms Shodeke (which did not though deal with the claims against Mr Hill). Ms Shodeke said that she required legal advice on the settlement terms and Mr Hill said that he also wanted to get legal advice and probably be represented by a barrister. Again albeit with some reluctance we agreed to an adjournment. We were not due to sit on the Monday so I directed that the case would next be heard on Tuesday 19 October 1999. I did however stress that all parties still remaining in the action after any settlement should be ready to proceed promptly at 10 a.m. on that day. Accordingly one week was to pass without the tribunal hearing any evidence at all.

On 19 October 1999 Ms Robertson, a barrister, appeared for the first time to represent Mr Hill. Mr Allen was there on behalf of the other respondents, but there was no Ms Shodeke. In fact Ms Shodeke had left a message with the tribunal office stating that she would be late as she was preparing some documents. We waited until 10.20 a.m. Mr Allen then said that he wished to apply to strike out all Ms Shodeke's claims. I said that the tribunal would be very reluctant to hear such an application in the absence of Ms Shodeke and that we would wait until 11 a.m. or Ms Shodeke's earlier arrival. In fact Ms Shodeke arrived shortly after eleven. Mr Allen said that he still wanted to make his application. Clearly the settlement negotiations had come to nothing. Mr Allen contended that the proceedings had been conducted by Ms Shodeke in a frivolous and vexatious manner (such being a basis for striking out a claim without hearing the evidence). Mr Allen submitted that Ms Shodeke had used the negotiations to settle to buy time and that it was frivolous and vexatious for her to turn up one hour late. Ms Robertson supported the application. Ms Shodeke denied that she had acted in bad faith and apologised for being late saying that she had been at home printing off two lengthy documents. We considered the application but decided to refuse to strike the cases out. However on Mr Allen's application we did order that Ms Shodeke should pay the Respondents' costs in respect of the time that had been wasted by her absence.

At about 11.45 a.m. on 19 October 1999 Ms Shodeke finally started giving her evidence and at last the action was really under way. Ms Shodeke continued giving her evidence on 20, 21 and 22 October 1999. At 3 p.m. on the 22nd however Ms Shodeke finished reading her witness statement and said that she was exhausted, was under stress and would like her cross examination to be put over to the following day. Conscious of the time we had lost and because we considered that Ms Shodeke was well enough to cope with one hour's cross examination, we refused the application. Ms Robertson therefore started to cross examine Ms Shodeke until 4 p.m.

By prior agreement there were no sittings on 25 to 29 October 1999.

On 1 November 1999 the tribunal had to deal with an application by Ms Shodeke about when the respondents should serve their witness statements on her. This took some time so that the cross examination of Ms Shodeke did not recommence until just after 11.30 a.m. This then went on for the rest of that day and continued on 2, 3, 4 and 5 November 1999.

On 8 November 1999 Ms Shodeke gave evidence by way of re-examination and in doing so produced some new documents. Mr Allen and Ms Robertson objected to the new documents being put in evidence and, after hearing the respective arguments, we agreed that the documents had no relevance to the issues in the case. A witness supporting Ms Shodeke's case then started to give her evidence, but we had to adjourn at about 2.30 p.m. because Ms Robertson was suffering from migraine.

On 9 November 1999 Ms Shodeke's witness continued giving her evidence until about 2.45 p.m. Mr Hill then started to give his evidence and this continued on 10, 11 and 12 November 1999.

No sittings took place on 15 to 18 November 1999 (if I remember correctly Mr Allen was appearing in another case in the House of Lords).

Three of the respondents' witnesses gave evidence on 19 November 1999, but we did not sit on 22 and 23 November 1999 because Mr Allen was again unavailable (another visit to the House of Lords I believe).

Mr Douglas gave evidence on 24 and 25 November 1999 and three more of the Respondents' witnesses gave evidence on 26 and 29 November 1999 finishing at about 12.45 p.m. It was accordingly convenient to take a slightly early lunch break and we informed Ms Shodeke that, as had been agreed by all parties the preceding Friday, we would hear her submissions as to why she should succeed after lunch. Ms Shodeke however said that she was not ready as she had had difficulty getting hold of the relevant law books from her library and she asked for an adjournment to Wednesday 1 December 1999. Mr Allen and Ms Robertson both opposed the application. The tribunal considered the various arguments, but decided to refuse the application. However as it was now 1.30 p.m. we agreed to extend the lunch break until 3 p.m. and we gave Ms Shodeke permission to use the tribunal library. We then sat until 5.45 p.m. because we were running out of sitting days and we wished to finish the hearing in the time still left to us.

30 November 1999 was a non- sitting day so that the parties could put the finishing touches to their submissions and we then sat on 1 and 2 December 1999 to hear the rest of those submissions.

The tribunal members met in chambers on 3 December 1999 and, after careful analysis of all the facts, concluded that there was no race discrimination and that the dismissal was not unfair. I then later sat at my desk at home and wrote up a 35 page decision which, after approval by my lay members, was sent to the parties on 17 January 2000.

I have set out the history of the hearing of the above action in some detail because it gives, I believe, an impression of the kind of difficulties faced by a tribunal in finishing a case within the time allotted – even when one has 26 days. All sorts of applications can be made and each one has to be listened to attentively and, after the three tribunal members have considered the arguments, a reasoned decision has to be given by the judge for its acceptance or refusal. This has to be recorded and later it has to form part of the final decision, because such decisions made during the hearing are open to appeal. Accordingly each application eats into the time allotted and makes it more difficult to finish on time. This can be frustrating, but applications during a hearing are part of the nature of litigation and the judge just has to show patience and accept that if a case overruns that is better than not giving the parties a fair opportunity to present their case properly. Of course - and I am here speaking generally – there are occasions when applications are deliberately made to use up time for one reason or another. That really is frustrating and difficult to deal with.

The factual backdrop to Ms Shodeke's case was very detailed. When it came to writing out the decision I note in looking back at it now that, after stating that Ms Shodeke commenced her employment as one of the principal officers in the children and families division of the authority in January 1994, I took 85 further paragraphs, each referring to a different date, to state the relevant facts. These paragraphs covered the period from 19 January 1996 to 22 May 1998, just over two years and four months – approximately three relevant facts per month.

In due course Ms Shodeke appealed against my tribunal's decision, putting forward 11 separate grounds - the bulk of these were to the effect that Ms Shodeke had not had a fair hearing, but she also appealed against the refusal to adjourn the hearing and the making of the order for costs. Ms Shodeke was now represented by a barrister. The appeal was heard by the Employment Appeal Tribunal and on 6 May 2004 judgment was given by the Employment Appeal Tribunal dismissing each and every ground put forward.

One ground of appeal that took me by surprise was the allegation that one of my lay members had fallen asleep at various times during the hearing and had not therefore heard all the evidence. This complaint had never been raised during the hearing and I had not noticed any lack of awareness by my colleague. It turned out that the lay member in question had a habit of shutting his eyes whilst concentrating and this had been possibly misconstrued. One of Ms Shodeke's witnesses to this behaviour described a particular afternoon when he alleged that my colleague was asleep. Fortunately my colleague was able to produce a full set of notes that he had taken that very afternoon, thereby proving that he was not asleep.

The judgment of the Employment Appeal Tribunal was even longer than my tribunal's decision, covering 59 pages. The four actions brought by Ms Shodeke, starting with her application presented on 22 January 1997, thus came to an end over seven years after they had started.

King v Abbey National plc and Others was an unusual case in a number of respects. Mr King was employed by the Abbey as a customer advisor from 27 November 2000 until 21

February 2001, a period of just under three months, when his contract came to an end. Mr King had then just turned 19 years of age. Mr King was complaining that he had suffered sexual discrimination and victimisation by three ladies who also worked for the Abbey. The case provoked some interest at the time because such allegations by men are, I believe, fairly rare. Mr King also gave an interview to the Evening Standard the day before the hearing was due to start and there was a detailed report of Mr King's allegations in that paper on the first day of the hearing. The court was full, there being a number of reporters present as well as the parties, their witnesses and their representatives. There were also television cameras outside the building. Mr King represented himself and the Abbey were represented by Miss R Jones, a solicitor.

Mr King made a number of allegations. Amongst these he contended that the three ladies discussed their sexual relationships in front of him, that two of them rubbed their breasts through their blouses in front of him, that one of them accused him of being a virgin, that one of them told him that he had a small penis, that two of them alleged that he was gay, that on one specific occasion two of the ladies jumped on top of each other and start kissing each other, that one lady lifted up her blouse in front of him and that another of the ladies tried on a new bra in front of him. Mr King's case was in effect that the events he had described took place so as to embarrass him. Mr King said that he was offended by such conduct.

On the second day of the hearing a very unusual event occurred. A brother of Mr King, who had read about the case in the newspapers, approached not Mr King himself but the Abbey and he told them that he wished to give evidence on their behalf. Miss Jones, the Abbey's solicitor, asked for leave to call the brother as a witness despite the lack of notice, but as there was insufficient time to hear his evidence that day we gave her provisional leave on the basis that the evidence was material and relevant and we directed her to obtain a written witness statement from the brother overnight. On the third day of the hearing the brother's witness statement was handed up to us together with two witness statements that Mr King had also obtained in anticipation of what his brother might say. In short, after reading all the witness statements, we considered that the evidence in the statements went to collateral matters and did not go to the issues in the case. Consequently my tribunal directed the parties that we did not wish to hear from any of these new witnesses.

During an internal investigation conducted by one of Abbey's managers one of the ladies admitted that she had told Mr King that he had a small dick and must be a virgin, but she claimed that this was in retaliation because Mr King had asked her if, when bathing her two boys aged five and one, she had got excited by washing their "willy wonkas" which she says shook her and made her angry. There was evidence that the three ladies did discuss their sexual lives at work but they claimed that it was only amongst themselves. Apart from these matters everything else was denied.

What sort of man then was Mr King? According to the evidence he danced like Michael Jackson during office hours and he kept a diary which contained a record of his dreams. In the decision we described Mr King as intelligent, self-possessed to the point of arrogance and attention seeking.

After hearing all the evidence and both sides' submissions, we concluded that Mr King had lied by either making up the incidents or taking an incident that did occur and exaggerating it to such an extent that it no longer bore any true resemblance to what actually happened. Mr King therefore lost his case and failed to become one of the few men to succeed in a case of sexual harassment by a woman or women.

Thinakaranathar v Tamil Community Housing Association Limited was a case that had some interesting aspects. The claimant was a Tamil who had been brought up as a Hindu but had later converted to Buddhism. When he was 36 the claimant married a Sinhalese lady who was a Buddhist. In October 1989 the claimant came to England to study at London University where he took a masters degree in urban development planning. The claimant's wife joined her husband in England in May 1990. The couple who had a limited permission to stay in England were due to return to Sri Lanka, but the claimant obtained political asylum on the grounds that if he returned to Sri Lanka he would be arrested at the airport as a suspected leader of the proscribed group known as the Tamil Tigers - a charge which he contended was totally untrue.

On 31 December 2000 the claimant applied for the position of a director with the respondents and in due course he was short listed with three others, a Tamil man, a white British man and a mixed race woman. Interviews were arranged to take place on 15 February 2001 but only the claimant and the Tamil man turned up. Both men presented written papers, made oral presentations and answered questions. The three person panel considered the merits of the two candidates and unanimously preferred the other Tamil man.

The claimant who was not happy with his rejection brought a tribunal claim alleging that the preference by the interview panel of the other Tamil man was due to race discrimination. The claimant was the better qualified of the two candidates and therefore he contended that his non selection was because his wife was Sinhalese. It should here be noted that the claimant was not relying on his own race, but that of his wife and secondly that both of the candidates were members of the same race, namely Tamils. The claimant's contention was perfectly arguable in law, but a very unusual situation nevertheless. Having heard all the evidence, my tribunal concluded that the interview panel genuinely believed that the other candidate was the better person for the job and we held that the race of the claimant's wife was not a factor in their decision. Accordingly the claimant lost his case.

Melhuish v Redbridge Citizens Advice Bureau was a case that threw up an interesting legal point, namely could a volunteer be an employee and thereby avail himself of employment rights such as the right not to be unfairly dismissed. Mr Melhuish worked for the CAB as a volunteer and was expected to attend the Bureau at least two days per week, later reduced to one day per week. However if Mr Melhuish did not want to work on a designated day he could ring up and cancel without any sanction. Mr Melhuish was paid his travelling expenses and was provided with free training. After six years service Mr Melhuish was informed by the Bureau that he could not any longer continue giving general advice to the public and he was offered alternative work. In those circumstances Mr Melhuish contended that he had been unfairly dismissed.

As already stated Mr Melhuish first had to show that he was an employee as defined by the relevant act of parliament which required that to be an employee there had to be a contract of employment in existence. Mr Melhuish submitted that there was a contract of employment that required him to attend on the days that had been agreed between him and the Bureau and that provided for his expenses and free training which amounted to remuneration. Thus said Mr Melhuish he was an employee. My tribunal first concluded, contrary to the Bureau's submission, that there was a contract between the parties, albeit not a contract of employment as such, but one limited to an obligation by the Bureau to repay proper expenses if they were incurred. We did not though accept Mr Melhuish's submission that he actually received remuneration. We held that if Mr Melhuish's expenses had been artificially inflated that might have made a difference and that if the training that he received was provided as recompense for work done that too might have made a difference, but neither was the case here.

After hearing submissions from Mr Melhuish and a solicitor representing the Bureau, my tribunal concluded broadly speaking that there was no contract of employment (and thus Mr Melhuish could not be an employee) firstly because there was no obligation on the Bureau to provide work nor any obligation on Mr Melhuish to carry out any work actually provided and secondly because Mr Melhuish did not receive any wage or other remuneration.

Mr Melluish was not prepared to accept that my tribunal had got it right and he appealed to the Employment Appeal Tribunal. Mr Melhuish again represented himself. The Employment Appeal Tribunal however came to the same conclusion as my tribunal, namely that there was no contract of employment. Accordingly the appeal was dismissed. The appeal judgment is now one of the leading authorities on the status of volunteers in employment law.

Focaroli v Bear, Stearns International Holdings Inc. and Others was, although lengthy, an interesting case. There were 14 witnesses and at the beginning of the hearing Bear, Stearns handed in to the tribunal nine lever arch folders containing all the relevant documents and numbering about 3000 pages. My tribunal sat for 12 days in March and April 2004 and we then considered our decision in chambers on 2 July 2004. I thereafter worked at home in writing up the decision which, after approval by my lay members, was typed up and covered

41 closely typed pages of A4 – one of the lengthiest of my career.

Mr Focaroli, an Italian gentleman, worked in a senior position for Bear, Stearns, a United States investment bank, for just over six years until he was dismissed on 4 July 2002. Mr Focaroli did not consider that he had been fairly treated and he brought proceedings against Bear, Stearns claiming unfair dismissal, disability discrimination and unlawful deduction from wages. Mr Focaroli, who with bonuses earned on average about two and a half million dollars a year, was seeking an award of over eight million dollars. Bear, Stearns disputed all of Mr Focaroli's claims apart from admitting that they had made an unlawful deduction from Mr Focaroli's wages. The main issue in the case was whether Mr Focaroli was a disabled person, namely a person who has "a physical or mental impairment which has a substantial and long-term adverse effect on his ability to carry out normal day-to-day activities." Mr Focaroli contended that he suffered from irritable bowel syndrome and an anxious depressive condition and was thus disabled.

Mr Focaroli went off sick near the beginning of February 2001 and he was still on sick leave in March 2002, over a year later. One of the key incidents in this case then occurred. The gentleman to whom Mr Focaroli reported, a Mr Brandolini, decided to take a skiing trip to St Moritz that month. On or about 25 March 2002 when he was out skiing Mr Brandolini was waiting at the top of a chair lift with two friends. Suddenly to Mr Brandolini's surprise Mr Focaroli came off the chair lift. Mr Brandolini said "hello, you look well" to which Mr Focaroli replied "so do you." Mr Brandolini then responded by saying "yes, but I am supposed to." Shortly after this wry comment Mr Focaroli skied off. On 23 May 2002 Bear, Stearns gave Mr Focaroli six weeks notice on the grounds of his continued incapability to perform his job.

My tribunal had to assess the evidence of all the witnesses and to read and consider the 3000 pages or so of relevant documents which included a large number of medical reports and medical records - amongst which were the reports of two jointly appointed experts. After careful analysis of all the evidence my tribunal concluded that Mr Focaroli was not a disabled person as defined by the Disability Discrimination Act 1995 at any material time and further that his dismissal was not unfair. Accordingly in those circumstances my tribunal did not have to consider the validity of the substantial claim for compensation which, if successful, would have been at that time one of the highest awards ever made by an employment tribunal.

Pye v Rosindell was a case that was interesting in a number of different ways. It was a claim of unfair dismissal by Miss Pye, a community assistant, against the M.P for whom she worked, a Mr Rosindell. Mr Rosindell who was a member of the conservative party was M.P. for Romford and at the time of the hearing had just been appointed shadow Minister for Home Affairs. Miss Pye was represented by a solicitor whom I shall call Mr A to save his blushes. Mr Rosindell however represented himself. Mr A contended that Miss Pye had been bullied into resigning her position and that accordingly such amounted to an unfair dismissal in law.

Pye v Rosindell is yet another case where the large number of applications made during the hearing made it impossible to finish the case in the time allotted to it. Three days had been allocated to the hearing which on reading the papers at the outset seemed enough to me. I was however in due course proved wrong. At the very beginning of the hearing Mr A said that the witness statements had been exchanged late, namely between 5 p.m. and 6 p.m. the previous evening. Because of this Mr A claimed that he needed an adjournment so that he could properly prepare his case. Mr Rosindell objected and asked for the case to proceed. I suggested that before deciding on this application we should all first try and identify the issues in the case. This we duly did and without explaining why Mr A withdrew his application and instead asked for a short break so that he could discuss with Miss Pye what he claimed to be new material in Mr Rosindell's witness statement. My tribunal agreed to this and the hearing resumed 45 minutes later. It was by now about 12.10 p.m. and Miss Pye started giving her evidence which was interrupted by us taking a lunch break at 1 p.m.

At 2p.m. Miss Pye was ready to continue giving evidence, but Mr A made an application that each tribunal member should declare whether he had any affinity or connection with the conservative party; he added that someone in court had informed him that every time the word "conservative" was mentioned the chairman had sat back and raised his eyebrow. Mr Rosindell said that he had not noticed any such behaviour himself and I added that I was unaware of any such reaction by me and that there was no reason why I should so react. Mr A then said that he wished to know if any tribunal member had any strong political interest in any of the other parties and how they voted. Mr A said that he was concerned that, if any of the tribunal members were staunch conservatives, they might not wish to find that a member of the shadow cabinet had unfairly dismissed his own employee. I told Mr A that I was not prepared to ask my colleagues how they voted, but we would consider the rest of his application in private. The lay members and I then retired to consider the application and on our return to court I told Mr A that I was not a member of any political party and that my colleagues had satisfied me that any political views they might have would not interfere with their duty to do justice in this case. On hearing this Mr A did not pursue the matter further and we continued to hear Miss Pye's evidence during the afternoon session.

About half way through the morning on the second day of the hearing, when Miss Pye was being cross examined by Mr Rosindell, Mr A made a further application. This was that a Mr Tebbutt who was present in court should be asked to leave because he had interfered with the witness, namely Miss Pye. I asked what the circumstances were and Mr A explained that he was in the court corridor when Mr Tebbutt approached him and told him that he was the worst solicitor he had ever seen. I asked Miss Pye if she had heard this remark and she said she had, but she confirmed that it would not change her evidence in any way. Accordingly we refused the application and Mr Tebbutt was not asked to leave the courtroom.

The third day was taken up with hearing more evidence and, although I tried to keep things moving, it was simply not possible to finish the case in the three days that had looked sufficient at the start.

As we had not made as much progress in Miss Pye's case as I would have liked, I decided to play safe and I booked a further four days with the listing office to complete the hearing. We were extremely fortunate to be able to obtain four days the following month as usually there would be a much larger gap.

During the break Mr A wrote in with a further application in which he applied for the hearing to be postponed. The reason given was that Mr A was involved in another case, but as it appeared that he was not actually the advocate in the other case his application was refused.

In due course my tribunal reassembled to continue hearing the case and in fact it took all of the four days reserved to finish hearing the rest of the evidence, the parties' submissions and to deliberate and give our judgment with reasons (due to a change in procedure decisions had now become judgments). In the end we held that Miss Pye had not in fact been unfairly dismissed by Mr Rosindell.

In looking back on the more unusual cases where I presided as chairman or later as judge I recall two both involving railwaymen which were factually interesting. One concerned an underground train driver whose train one day would not move out of the station because the doors in one of the carriages would not shut. The driver therefore got out of the train and pushed the doors shut. The problem resolved the train duly took off, but unfortunately without the driver. I believe the train went through three or four stations before the power was cut off and it came to an abrupt halt. If I recall correctly the driver claimed that he had hung a bag of tools on the brake (a dead man's handle) which must have fallen off. The driver's employers said, even if true, that this was an unauthorised and dangerous short cut and they dismissed him. We considered that the employers were justified in bringing the contract to an end and the claimant accordingly lost his case of unfair dismissal.

The other case involving a railwayman concerned a male sleeping car attendant who was scheduled to travel to Edinburgh on, if I recall correctly, one particular Christmas Eve. Having carried out his duties, the attendant was entitled to return home on his own and he accordingly boarded what he thought was the train to London, but in fact the train he got on was going not to London but to Aberdeen. The weather was not good - it was in fact snowing - and the train made a temporary stop shortly after leaving Edinburgh station and the attendant, after speaking to another passenger, then discovered that he was on the wrong train. The attendant told the tribunal that the front of the train had just entered a tunnel, but that he was able to walk to the back of the train and get off. The attendant said that by going to the rear of the train he was able to alight on the station platform, but the railway company produced compelling evidence that their longest train on that particular line was in fact considerably shorter than the distance from the end of the platform to the beginning of the tunnel. We accepted this evidence and concluded that the railwayman had in fact walked on what were snow covered railway tracks in the dark - a very dangerous manoeuvre. As the claimant was responsible for the safety of the passengers in his sleeping car we agreed with his employers that he had not shown proper regard for his own safety and could not therefore be trusted with the safety of others. This railwayman too lost his claim that he had been unfairly dismissed.

Another case that I recollect because of the somewhat unusual facts was that of a young postman who had a date with his girlfriend on Hampstead Heath. Unfortunately when the time arrived for him to meet his girlfriend the young man had not finished delivering all of his letters, so his solution to this dilemma was to stash the undelivered letters in a bush on the Heath. When this was discovered the young man's manager was not at all sympathetic to his plight and dismissed him, but instead of taking his medicine the young man brought a claim that he had been unfairly dismissed as it was his first offence. I cannot now recall the discussions I had with my lay members, but I do recall that we dismissed the young man's claim.

One case I remember well had a somewhat dramatic ending. The lady who was bringing the case and representing herself was making her closing submissions. These have to be based on the evidence actually given and it is not permissible for new facts to be introduced as this would be unfair to the other party who would not have had the opportunity to cross examine any witness about them. At the very beginning of her submissions the lady claimant said "As is well known I suffer from asthma…" I intervened and said "I am sorry, but no evidence was called as to that and you cannot make it part of your submissions." The claimant then started to gasp and her body heaved. The lady was having an attack of some sort - quite possibly asthmatic. I called for medical assistance and the lady was given attention by a first aid officer who I think gave her oxygen. About half an hour later the lady had fully recovered and I invited her to make her submissions from the start. "As is well known I suffer from asthma..." she said. I let it go this second time. After all we could simply ignore it and I did not want her to have another attack, asthmatic or otherwise.

There were I am sure many other dramatic or humorous occurrences in court that I have now forgotten. It is after all a somewhat theatrical occasion, even though we are all dressed in normal, albeit somewhat formal, attire. The case though that I sat on which for a time anyway had the greatest impact on the law is the saga involving Mr Rutherford and Mr Bentley, which I shall summarise in the following paragraphs.

The case of Rutherford v Harvest Town Circle Limited was initially listed to be heard by my tribunal in January 1999 but we adjourned it until the European Court had given its decision in another case that was likely to be relevant to Mr Rutherford's case. We reassembled in July 1999 after the European Court had given its decision in the other case. Mr Rutherford who was 67 at the time had been dismissed by Harvest Town Circle Limited on the grounds of redundancy. Mr Rutherford was aggrieved and he therefore brought a claim seeking compensation for unfair dismissal and a redundancy payment. The difficulty Mr Rutherford however faced was that the Employment Rights Act 1996 provided a cut-off date of 65 in respect of both heads of claim and age discrimination, which might have helped Mr Rutherford, was then still some seven years ahead. An interesting and ingenious argument was though put forward on Mr Rutherford's behalf. This was that the provisions in the 1996

Act were in fact contrary to Article 141 of the Treaty of Rome and should therefore be disregarded as being incompatible with European law. The legal issues in this case are complex but suffice for now to say Mr Rutherford had first to prove that there was indirect sex discrimination, namely this is so "where an apparently neutral provision, criterion or practice disadvantages a substantially higher proportion of the members of one sex unless that provision, criterion or practice is appropriate and necessary and can be justified by objective factors unrelated to sex." Mr Rutherford was contending that a "substantially higher proportion" of men were affected by the cut-off date than were women.

To decide the case we had to look at a large number of statistics and in doing so we concentrated on those relating to men and women aged over 65. By example in 1998, the year of the dismissal, of just over five million women aged over 65 3% were economically active whereas of just over three and a half million men aged over 65 8% were economically active. In analysing the figures we came to the conclusion that a substantially higher proportion of males were disadvantaged by the cut-off date than were women and as there was no evidence put before us of objective justification we held that Mr Rutherford could proceed with his claim. I cannot though claim that my tribunal was the first to decide this point as a similar case had been heard by a tribunal sitting in Croydon and they too had found in favour of the employee.

Mr Rutherford's employers appealed to the Employment Appeal Tribunal and in July 2001 Mr Justice Lindsay gave his Tribunal's judgment. In short Mr Justice Lindsay considered that the statistics we had analysed were inadequate for our purpose and that the Secretary of State should be invited to join in the proceedings. The judgment did not state what statistics would be appropriate, but it did give some guidelines.

221

A Mr Bentley, who was raising similar arguments in a different case, and the Secretary of State for Trade and Industry were joined as parties in the Rutherford case and the revised action was listed to be heard by me again albeit with different lay members. The applicants' legal team was now led by Mr Robin Allen Q.C. (the barrister who appeared in the Shodeke case) and the Secretary of State's legal team was led by Mrs Melanie Hall Q.C. My tribunal sat for five days in June 2002 and four days in July 2002. I then worked in my study at home and prepared in longhand a draft decision in which I set out the history of the proceedings, the facts, which were not in dispute, and the applicable law. I then met up with my lay members at a chambers meeting in August 2002 and we spent a packed day going through all of the issues in the case and I spent further time in my study writing up the final document, which was duly approved by my lay members. Following this a 20 page decision was sent out to the parties.

During the hearing of the Rutherford/Bentley case my tribunal were presented with a large number of statistics which were explained to us by experts. One of the main arguments on the statistics was whether we should concentrate on all employees in England and Wales with one, or two, year service (the qualifying periods for unfair dismissal and redundancy respectively) who were no younger than 16 and no older than 79 (one of Mrs Hall's contentions) or on some other group. We however pointed out that those employees with one or two years service aged 16 to 17 might by the time they reached 65 (if they ever did) be in employment with more or less than one year service, be self- employed, be too ill to work at all, be unemployed, be in retirement or have emigrated. We therefore concluded that statistics of persons working, seeking work or wanting to work and covering age bands that were closer to the age of 65 were more appropriate. We accordingly looked in particular at various bands covering the period from ages 55 to 74. We also considered the numbers, the percentages, the percentage point differences and the ratios – a complex task. On analysis we then concluded that the cut-off date in the legislation did disadvantage a substantially higher proportion of men than women. We also found in favour of the applicants in holding that the discrimination was not justified by objective factors unrelated to sex. Accordingly we held that Mr Rutherford and Mr Bentley could proceed with their claims. Unusually for a decision by an employment tribunal this case was reported in the official law reports.

Whilst I was grappling with the intricacies of the Rutherford/Bentley case employees aged over 65 who had been dismissed were waiting on my tribunal's decision. When that decision was given these employees realised that they might have a case after all and they started or continued proceedings in employment tribunals all over England and Wales. These cases were however put on hold as the State indicated that it would appeal against my tribunal's decision.

The State did in fact appeal and the appeal to the Employment Appeal Tribunal was heard in May 2003 and a judgment 80 pages long was delivered in October 2003 allowing the appeal. In particular the Employment Appeal Tribunal held that my tribunal erred in taking as the relevant pool for comparison those between age 55 and 74 and in excluding the pool advanced by the Secretary of State of employees aged 16 to 79.

Mr Rutherford and Mr Bentley did not leave matters there and they appealed to the Court of Appeal. Unfortunately for them the three judges comprising that Court took a similar view to the Employment Appeal Tribunal and in September 2004 they dismissed the appeal.

Still Mr Rutherford and Mr Bentley did not give up and they appealed to the House of Lords. In May 2006 the House of Lords, consisting of five Law Lords, dismissed the appeal. The majority of the House of Lords did not agree with the Court of Appeal's reasoning and somewhat ironically, in view of the emphasis so far placed on the assistance that statistics provided, decided that the statistics were in effect irrelevant. Their Lordships held that since the statutory bar applied to everyone aged over 65 and could apply to nobody under that age it did not disadvantage a higher proportion of the members of one sex than of the other. The appeal was accordingly dismissed.

Accordingly Mr Rutherford, who had been dismissed in October 1998, had taken well over seven years to find out that he had no right to put forward his claims for compensation after all.

Although I had the dubious pleasure of reading the judgments of four different courts in the Rutherford/Bentley litigation all stating that I and my colleagues had got it wrong I nevertheless found my participation in the two hearings a very stimulating and interesting experience.

On 31 August 2008 my term of appointment as an employment judge expired and on Friday 29 August 2008, the last sitting day of that month, I sat on my last case. I was over 72 years of age and subject to compulsory retirement. Age discrimination was now against the law, but no, I did not bring any case against the State!

In considering my time working within the employment tribunal system my impression is that the system worked and overall worked well. Except for the heavy cases, hearings generally took place within a reasonable time from a claim being made and a reasonably intelligent person could present their own case with some help from the judge, provided that there were no difficult legal issues in it. Many lawyers supplied their services free to claimants and generally legal costs, when incurred, were reasonably proportionate to what was at stake. When I was sitting an employee or worker could start proceedings without having to pay any fee, and inevitably some disgruntled employees or workers took advantage of the system and brought hopeless cases that involved the respondents in legal costs and loss of personnel from their posts whilst they were giving evidence in the tribunal. In such cases the tribunal has the power to order the claimant to pay the respondents' legal costs and such orders, I believe, are being made more often than used to be the case, but that is no guarantee that any money will actually be received. The difficulty with costs orders is that claimants with legitimate claims, whether they win or lose in the end, should not be put off bringing a case because they might have to pay the other side's costs. It should also be remembered that many of the claimants will have just lost their job and be short of money themselves. I on a number of occasions became aware of cases where the employers or their representatives had frightened the claimant into abandoning a potentially winnable case by informing him or her that if a claim was brought or pursued they would seek a substantial order for costs against them. This is clearly not right. However the balance in my view is not easy to strike.

Now that I am fully retired from the law I am trying to improve my golf. I always used to think that it was only the fact that I could not play as often as I liked that was holding me back. Unfortunately, having now been fully retired for over six years, my handicap has gone in the wrong direction and I am therefore having to face up to the fact that I am just not a very good golfer after all. However playing golf provides good companions to talk to and good exercise in the open air. Furthermore most golf courses, including my home

225

course, are very pleasant places to take a walk even if this requires, as it does in my case, regular visits into prickly gorse bushes or thick and tangled heather.

Looking back on my professional life I consider that I was very lucky in that I enjoyed being a lawyer, whether practising as a solicitor or sitting as a judge in the employment tribunals. I was also exceptionally lucky as a part time judge to preside over a number of cases that involved important points of law.

Now that I have retired from both jobs I miss the contrast between work and play and in particular the stimulus of going into court without knowing what I am going to experience on that particular day. Is it going to be a relatively straightforward case or will I get a difficult litigant in person or a tricky point of law? What I also miss but gladly so are the long commutes and the early rises.

In writing this book I have been able to relive some interesting, some amusing and some embarrassing experiences. I hope that I have also entertained my readers.

Printed in Great Britain
by Amazon

24207441R00126